The Complete Guide to House Flipping & Real Estate

This Go To Guide Shows You How To Achieve Financial Freedom Through Property Investing Including Rental, Commercial, Marketing, House Flipping And More

By David Hewitt & Andrew Peter

"The Complete Guide to House Flipping & Real Estate: This Go To Guide Shows You How To Achieve Financial Freedom Through Property Investing Including Rental, Commercial, Marketing, House Flipping And More" Written by "David Hewitt & Andrew Peter".

The Complete Guide to House Flipping & Real Estate is a bundle of the books "Real Estate Investing Beginners Guide" & "House Flipping– Beginners Guide".

Hope You Enjoy!

By reading this document, the reader agrees that under no circumstances is the author responsible for any losses, direct or indirect, that are incurred as a result of the use of the information contained within this document, including, but not limited to, errors, omissions, or inaccuracies.

Table of Contents

Real Estate Investing Beginners Guide

Learn the ABCs of Real Estate for Becoming a Successful Investor! Make Passive Income with Rental Property, Commercial, Marketing, and Credit Repair Now!

David Hewitt & Andrew Peter

Introduction

When it comes to powerful investment opportunities, real estate is the most time-tested of all ways, having been successfully converting a profit as long as the idea of land ownership is active. Therefore, it is one of the robust asset types that professional's advice for any portfolio regardless of whether the holder is just getting started or looking to diversify.

It provides numerous benefits when it comes to profitability, liquidity, diversification, and cash flow if you are looking for a way to learn how to get started in real estate investing, this book will teach you how to become a real estate investing guru.

Inside, you'll learn everything you wanted to learn about real estate investment, including how to get started with a little amount of capital, or if you have a bad credit score. You will also learn how to locate the best properties that deserve little to no work before they can be listed for sale. You will also gain an in-depth method for success regardless of whether you want to buy a property and hold onto it for the long-term or if you're more interested in house flipping.

Real estate investing is the first step that many people dive in to attain financial freedom. And this book presents you with secrets that you can follow to become successful, like the best real estate investors. So, what are you waiting for? Keep reading to unlock your financial future.

Chapter 1: The Two Most Common Questions

How Do I Get Started in Real Estate Investing?

Most people interested in getting started in real estate investing don't know how to get started. While there is no perfect time to start real estate investing, it is also good to do your due diligence, do enough research, run numbers, become creative, and be ready to take calculated risks to succeed. If you're ready to face the challenge, then it is time to discover how to get started in real estate.

First, let us debunk some myths about real estate investing

1. It's Not Meant for Me

Well, if you think real estate investments are only for rich people who can take risks because they don't have hungry mouths to feed, then you're wrong. Think twice. Single moms, women, divorced- are all buying lands and profiting from this real estate boom.

It doesn't matter how much money you can afford, even with the little you have, you can still start small. And that's even better because there's a lot to learn and lots of mistakes to be made. The smaller the investment, the less costly the mistake.

2. Only Men Can Succeed in Real Estate

Anybody can succeed in real estate. In fact, women have a higher percentage of being successful than men.

3. The Market May Change

Once you learn how to get started in real estate, you will begin to understand that the market doesn't matter so much. Real estate investment works in any place, and for anyone who invests their energy, time, and interest in getting started.

Many first-time investors lose their cash after investing in real estate. But this only happens to those who don't understand the rubrics of purchasing and selling real estate. Therefore, this reveals that the right way to get started in this niche is by acquiring the relevant knowledge in all areas of real estate investing. To help you out in your journey to become a real estate investor, we have briefly highlighted the main areas that you need to know as a beginner. An extensive discussion of these topics will be explored in the coming chapters.

Select the Right Investment Location

Where you purchase your first investment property determines the amount of profit you can expect. This is the reason first-time real estate investors must consider the location of a property. For example, you can get a good rental property for sale at an affordable price, but the neighborhood isn't so great. Based on several factors, buying this rental might not be the best move for making more returns in real estate investing. Some of these factors include:

- Rental rates and monthly income
- Supply and demand rates
- Crime rates and safety
- Operating costs and expenses
- Real estate appreciation trends

All of these factors determine the amount of profit a location may generate, and how profitable investment properties in a particular location are. So, the advice for investors launching a rental property business is always to monitor the trends that affect the housing market before you invest your money on a property. The best places to invest in real estate will generate a high rental income, good return on investment, and positive cash flow.

Choose Your Rental Strategy

Most people, when they come across the term rental properties, their minds shift to apartments and houses that are rented out to long-term tenants. This is the traditional rental strategy, and it's has been running for decades; that is why it is the most popular method of investing in real estate. However, there is another rental strategy that has emerged in the last few years, and it's beginning to become the best strategy in real estate investing. The short-term rental strategy implies that real estate investors purchase vacation homes to rent out to guests for a short period.

Finding Your Investment Property

There are many kinds of investment properties that you can select from for getting started in real estate. There is a small apartment, single-family homes, townhomes, and many more. Deciding on the type of property you want as your first investment will allow you to narrow down your search results until you get the perfect one. Since you're a beginner real estate investor, our recommendation is to start small.

Perform a Real Estate Market Analysis

Once you find a house for sale, the next thing is to do your market analysis. Don't be quick to buy it. Not every house will generate profit as a rental property, and as an investor, you don't want to invest your money on a property that doesn't earn you a profit. The only way to determine the profitability of an investment property is running a real estate market analysis.

This is the procedure for evaluating investment opportunities to determine the expected profit and risks. It offers investors with a detailed picture of the location, and the profit you expect to make from investing. In general, real estate market analysis helps you evaluate the property and compare it to similar ones in the market to see if purchasing it makes financial sense and generates profits.

Financing Your Investment Property

After you are done analyzing the property, now it's time to take ownership of the investment property. One major concern of real estate investing for first-time investors is financing. Some believe that investors only buy properties with money, but the fact is, not all do. One of the rewards of investing in real estate is that you can borrow other people's money to make money. This is a great way to begin in real estate, investing with little cash. We shall learn more about financing your investment property in the coming chapters. For now, this is what you need to know when you want to become a real estate investor.

Why You Should Choose Real Estate Investing

When you get a chance for growth in business or a salary increment, you can be tempted to use your wealth to buy things for yourself. However, if you are financially wise, you know you would better use your extra money on something that would generate more value in the long-term.

Real estate properties are a great source of strong and stable investment. A great investment is one that you would spend most of your cash on but would generate more in return.

There are many areas where you can invest your money: such as in stocks and bonds. But still, the advantages of real estate investments are higher than any other type of investment.

Here are the best reasons why you should choose to invest in real estate properties:

It Is a Secure Financial Investment

Real estate properties increase in value at a rate that would go for up to 3% per year. Their value does not depend much on external factors, unlike other investment types. Political instability, wat, or disaster does not affect the odds of land properties to add their worth.

Also, there is a lower risk for real estate properties. Unlike the stock markets where they can easily be destroyed in a few minutes because of their high market volatility, real estate does not cause that kind of threat.

You Can Leverage

Since real estate is a physical property, it is easy to get financing to purchase it. This is what is referred to as "leveraging." This is not the same as purchasing "shares."

Also, you can rent off your property. The income you earn from the rent can be used to clear the remaining fee of your property.

In other words, you don't need to bring all the capital from your storehouse to buy the property.

Its Value Always Appreciates over Time

The longer you hold on to your land or building, the higher its cost increases. The rate at which the value rise might depend on several factors, but history indicates that real estate property increases in value every year.

It is Simple

Investing in stock markets would demand a lot of studies. Some might even hire experts to do the researching for them. But when it comes to purchasing properties, you don't need to go through problems like that.

With some help from experts, you can choose the property of your choice. Besides, some of those who would get their homes have initially considered living in them. The realization of gaining from their acquisition would come later when they are aware of the growth of the property's price.

It Generates Passive Income

There multiple ways to earn income from real estate property. It depends on what you would like to do. First, you can wait longer to construct a retirement home. That way, the value of the house is going to appreciate.

Another way is to set a higher rental fee than the holding price. One way of achieving this is a moderate investment in middle-class condominium around commercial areas where workers can rent in your condo.

Another method is to buy old or almost dilapidated properties at a cheaper amount, then improve the place and sell it at a higher cost.

Whatever you decide with your real estate property, you can sit back and allow your money to work for you. The best thing you can have is time. With passive income, you can use your time for things that are crucial to you, and this raises the quality of your life.

It Is a Usable Asset

The best thing about buying your own house is you can live inside. You can decide to use it for your own good. This is different from owning a bar of gold where you don't have the luxury of using them.

You Can Control It

Once you own the asset, you have total control over what to do with it. You can choose to increase the rent, or you can use your place.

It Has Tax Benefits

The accumulating value of your real estate isn't taxed unless your property is aging. This means if you own more real estate properties, there is a higher chance of multiplying your property value. With real estate, you have numerous opportunities for your money to increase without the threat of being taxed.

In summary, if you invest in real estate properties, you will, for sure, reap the benefits of the growth of your fortune. We constantly look for new methods to make money through a business, investment, or in any other way. Real estate investing is one of the best ways to realize that goal.

Chapter 2: FAQs Every Real Estate Beginner Wants to Know

Can I Get Involved in Real Estate if I Have a Full-Time Job?

Yes, and the sooner you start, the better.

Most people think that to be successful in real estate investing, they need to quit their job and work full-time as real estate investors. It's a difficult decision to make because there are many advantages to maintaining your job as well as drawbacks to consider.

Here's what you need to know.

There are numerous ways to generate money in real estate, and each strategy and technique differs in the amount of time required.

Some methods may require you to become active in your business, and others may require 40 hours per week. Other ways can be more passive and require a total of 40 hours all year.

The good thing about real estate is the variety of choices available and building a business that fits your lifestyle, experience, financial situation, goals, and education.

Having a Job Increases Growth in Your Investing Business

One of the major reasons to invest in real estate while you have a job is that your job can provide you with the income you want to support your investment business.

Depending on the amount of money you save, you'll have money every year to direct in real estate investments.

You'll also manage to reinvest the money from your investments because you'll use your job salary to cater to your cost of living.

A person who invests full time and has no other job might experience slower growth because they have to use the income from their investments to finance living expenses.

A Job Will Help You Get Financing from a Bank

Another reason to not quit your job when you're first starting in real estate investing is the availability of bank finance. To receive a loan from a bank, you need to submit evidence of your income and have a great credit score.

Your job will be proof of the amount of income you qualify for bank financing.

In most cases, entrepreneurs and investors who don't have a 9-5 job and work full time as real estate investors find it difficult to qualify for loans from banks because their business isn't generating sufficient income yet, or they lack 2-3 years proof of stable income.

In short, your job will be a great tool in the early stages of launching your real estate business. This will go on until the ball gets rolling, and your business operates well enough to help you quit.

All in all, your full-time job should not discourage you from starting to invest in real estate. You have to be more adaptable to work with the free time you have, but it's doable.

Overall, if you have a job with flexible hours or can take long breaks, it's going to be a little easier to get started.

For those having a standard one-hour lunch break and full workday, your weekends, nights, and lunch breaks are going to be when you have to commit to your investing business.

Of course, these won't be the best times to meet with sellers, but you can work on other elements of your business during off periods. Make the most out of your free time.

Do I Need to Hire a Professional to Become Successful?

With the numerous number of mentorship programs launched online daily, it's very easy for first-time investors to get the wrong perception that they need a real estate guru to register success. However, the fact is that you don't need one to be successful. In fact, many of the successful real estate investors were self-made men. They did not hire a real estate guru to be successful.

It also helps to remember that many of the so-called real estate gurus you will find online are requesting you to pay a huge sum in exchange for things that are too good to be true. You know them: they sell you in on the promise of quick riches, easy money, early retirement as a millionaire, and so forth.

And you can easily tell the kind of services they offer. It's almost always methods that are stuck behind different paywalls:

- Bootcamps

- Expensive courses
- Online coaching
- Seminars
- Mentorship programs

You can easily tell that most of the strategies being sold are already well-documented and available for free somewhere else on the internet.

You also need to track the money trail. It's not just these experts that profit from their marketing services. Many affiliate marketers market and resell these services in exchange for a certain commission.

For sure, you don't have to hire a Real Estate Guru to succeed.

You will attain the required perspective if you explore these guru's business model: you don't really have any evidence that they are making a profit from all the strategies, tactics, techniques, and tricks they are teaching you. Instead, it sounds more like they accumulate all of their money from mentoring subscriptions, subscription fees, eBook sales, and seminar tickets. If you look at it from that angle, it appears more like a con than a secret to success.

That said, these gurus aren't all snake oil salesmen. Some of them are knowledgeable and are amazing salesmen, businessmen, and marketers. The biggest challenge is that you're likely to find a guru who just wants to con you as you are of getting an actual mentor.

The most important thing is that you don't need to spend thousands of dollars on these gurus. You can get most of the information they teach all over the internet, for free. You might find genuine mentors out there, but you need to be careful all the time and avoid being gullible. As a real estate investor, you must be skeptic, and this is a skill that you will have to learn on your own.

Can I Invest in Real Estate Without Money?

Put simply, yes. If you want to invest in real estate without money, you need to develop a means to recognize, understand, and even use other people's money. Still, you will need some money to pay a down payment, when you choose to finance real estate through conventional loans.

Investing in real estate by using other people's money is a genuine approach for some of the best real estate investing businesses.

For the financially troubled investors and the new investors, investing in real estate without any money is a great way of testing the waters.

While you can invest in real estate with no money, but if you don't have any money, you will need to look for other strategies to contribute resources. Remember, there are a million ways to drive a real estate deal, and you cannot bring money to the deal, then what else can you bring. The answer here is if you want to invest in real estate with no money, then go search for people that have money and make it worth for them to put their money to work with you.

Can I Invest in Real Estate When I Have a Bad Credit?

Buying or owning an investment property is one of the best ways to attain long-term wealth. However, the most common problem that real estate investors experience when financing investment properties are being ineligible for bank loans because mortgage lenders usually avoid lending money to real estate investors with a poor credit score. But that doesn't mean there are no other means to finance an investment property.

What Is a Bad Credit Score?

A credit score refers to a statistical number that determines an individual's creditworthiness. Mortgage lenders rely on credit scores to determine whether to give a person a loan and at which interest rate the loan is released. Put simply; a high credit score indicates the person is financially trustworthy to pay back a loan. For real estate investors, a good credit score is the best situation because it qualifies them for loans at lower interest rates and better terms. On the other hand, a bad score might mean a loan is not an option.

Your credit score is computed based on an analysis of your credit files. Whether you like it or not, this number reveals the probability that you will pay your bills. If you are among the unlucky ones, a bad credit score doesn't really mean you cannot purchase an investment property.

So, you can still invest in real estate with a bad credit score.

How to Get Around a Bad Credit Score and Still Invest in Real Estate

A bad credit score doesn't mean you cannot buy property as an investment.

1. Buy a Rehab

Real estate investors with low credit scores might not qualify for loans that would cover the price of a single-family property. But they may still qualify for a loan that would help fix a distressed property. This type of investment property can be improved and flipped for a profit. Fix, and flip is a short-term real estate investment method that generates high profit in a short period if done correctly. The only drawback of this investment method is that you'll need to invest in a lot of effort for the best results. Sometimes, new costs emerge as you move on with the flipping project.

2.   Get a Co-Signer

If you think you have the best investment property but don't have good credit that qualifies you for a loan, then find someone to co-sign who will be a guarantor for your loan. Requesting a close friend or family member with a good credit score to co-sign your rental property mortgage is a great idea as long as you ensure you pay your mortgage payments. Failing to do so will not only worsen your credit score, but that of your co-signer too.

3.   Create a Partnership

Creating a real estate partnership is a great way to make use of another's personal credit to drive a real estate investment opportunity. The only difference in this method is that you have to divide any profits with your partner. Building a real estate partnership provides many advantages; collecting resources can help you achieve a huge investment property and extend your real estate investing network. However, a poorly planned partnership can become a problem, particularly in the absence of a partnership contract. For that reason, it is better to sign a contract when forming a partnership.

4.   Hard Money Lenders

If you're still thinking of how you can buy an investment property with a bad credit score, then hard money is your best option. Hard money lenders are businesses that lend money at high-interest rates. Besides that, hard money lenders charge a huge amount of fees, which makes them unfavorable for long-term real estate investments. However, hard money is perfect for a fix and flip investment method. This way, a real estate investor can borrow hard money, generate profit, and move on to the next project. Getting a hard money loan using a bad credit score isn't a problem because hard money lenders don't have to stick to regulations and lending policies of banks.

Overall, if you want to buy an investment property using a bad credit score, the best way is to improve your credit score first. A good credit score will qualify you for loans at lower interest rates and better terms. But if you think you have what it takes to make it in real estate investing, but you are affected with a bad credit score, consider the above strategies.

Is Real Estate Investing a Get Rich Quick Scheme?

About half of all new investors don't go past their first year. The reason for this lack of knowledge is because they think the business is easier than it really is. The multiple real estate flipping shows on TV sets a rosy picture of the investing business. If you watch these shows, it would appear that all you need to do is get a property you like, do some little work, and wait for the buyer to come along. Anyone who is in the business knows this is a lie. Overall, real estate investing isn't a "get rich quick" scheme. It demands a lot of hard work and commitment.

There are obstacles in every sector of the business. Even under the right conditions with the best scenario, it still requires months to buy and sell a property. Wholesaling can be done quicker, but will not generate the profit new investors want. When all is said and done, once all the expenses and obligations are paid for, the final say on every deal might leave new investors feeling less thrilled. They think they will hit a home run on each deal, but the truth is that most real estate investing involves hitting singles and doubles, and waiting for the perfect chance to take a big swing.

The profit from every deal might be less than expected, and the work more than the earlier discussed. This is how investing business happens. If you think you are going to hit the ground running with a dozen closings and a net worth of million dollars, you're not molded in reality. The real estate business can be very lucrative, but again it takes time and hard work to build. If you don't see instant results, it can be easy to believe the isn't for you, or you don't have the passion it takes to become successful.

Overnight success takes years to happen. Most investors have been in the business for years until getting a niche or a contact that allows their business to grow. The thought of earning more from a single deal than it was in the previous job is interesting, but that is not the norm. The truth is that you may need to spend the time to run a mail campaign. You might speak to 10 homeowners just to strike one deal. They don't indicate this on TV, but this is where you get your business. Even after you reach this point, you still need to handle rehab costs, buyer issues, and budgeting problems before you get to the closing. There is a lot of opportunity in investing, but it also comes with a lot of perseverance and hard work.

If you have a genuine passion for real estate, you can be successful in a shorter period, but even that will not happen in the first 30 days. There is no get-rich-quick scheme in real estate. Investing requires education and hard work.

What If My Niche Is Too Expensive?

If you're considering buying a home, but left disappointed by increasing prices in your community, you're not alone. This happens all over.

When you are saving up for a down payment and wondering through your financial choices, increasing home prices can add pressure. It's tempting to seek creative financing options or justify spending more than you can manage to secure a home. But don't something silly!

Before you step into financial disaster, understand that you have other choices that don't eat your budget.

Here are some ways to find a home even when the market is too expensive

1. Set Boundaries for Your Home Prices

Start by setting limits for your finances. Before you can screen your options, you must know how much you can afford to pay for a house. How much home you can afford should be depending on your financial status, not pressure triggered by the prices in your housing market.

If you cannot pay cash for your property, the best choice is a mortgage loan done correctly.

2. Spread Your Search

You might want to live in a city, or maybe you have concentrated on suburban life, but increasing your search may change your mind about where you really want to be. Home prices are always more affordable outside the metro zone.

You could be stuck in a market where homeownership will always appear out of reach. However, if you're open to moving, relocating can quickly boost your home-buying dream. Young entrepreneurs are using this approach.

Is It a Must to Have LLC or a Corporation to Invest in Real Estate?

No. It's not mandatory to have an LLC. An LLC may provide limited protection, and it will never safeguard you from criminal acts if you are ready to maintain the required records and operate correctly. If you're aren't, the LLC can easily be pierced. Probably, many real estate investors don't bother to maintain enough records. Their LLCs might be worse. Those investors work under the mistaken notion that their assets are safeguarded but may realize shortly after they are linked to a lawsuit.

An LLC might be difficult to represent yourself in court. Most district courts need entities to be represented by an attorney. Simple landlord-tenant disputes which an individual landlord can rule can quickly become more expensive and time-consuming if their rental property is an LLC.

Don't forget that when an attorney suggests that you get an LLC, they have a chance to profit from setting up the entity and the additional work-related with maintaining them. There are yearly filings and extra tax work required. In some situations, the attorney may have little to no experience with ownership of a rental property.

The main thing is that the perceived security of an LLC can easily be destroyed, especially if you are an owner-manager. Get a loan in your personal name to buy the property, and you just destroyed the LLC. It is impossible to attain conventional financing in an LLC, so this is what most people do.

From a practical point of view, most people getting started in real estate have very little to secure. Even if you have several rental properties, the probability is that the bank owns 80% of the property, so you don't necessarily own it. They cannot take something you don't own. Obviously, there is always bankruptcy if something freak occurs. They cannot take your retirement accounts, which is where most people store wealth.

Should I Wait to Invest Until the Market Changes?

Most real estate investors and prospective real estate investors understand that an increase in housing prices will finally result in a massive drop. These investors are worried about buying anything and think that they can get a better deal when everything drops.

First, it's hard to know whether there will be another market crash. Many investors assume there will be another market crash. However, an increase in price doesn't mean the housing market crash. In fact, if you base on the historical housing market index, prices aren't higher than average trends. They appear higher because we experienced a huge drop and then a rapid rise in a short time. If you check the historical graph of the housing price index, we aren't far from normal.

If you are waiting for the market to change in housing prices, how long will you wait? Will you leave your money to sit for one year, two, four, or more?

Suppose the market you are waiting to invest in never drops. There's no guarantee that each market will drop, or how far it will drop. In summary, there will always be opportunities in real estate, but it might not be easy to identify that opportunity exactly. So rather than wait for the perfect market, think of the kind of opportunities available in the current market.

Is It a Must to Have a Real Estate License?

This is a common question you hear when someone wants to become a real estate investor. While owning a license can be helpful to your real estate investing career, you don't really need one if you want to become a real estate investor. In fact, there are no licensing requirements at the state level of people who invest in real estate. A license would be mandatory if you were to become a real estate agent. However, many investors choose to get a real estate license because of its many benefits.

So, that takes us to the next question. How can you become a real estate investor without a license?

Well, here are useful tips and tools that you can use to become a successful investor without getting a license.

Four Things You Need

1.   Education

Educating yourself on real estate investing is important to ensure you succeed. You must have enough knowledge of all the features of real estate investing.

2.   Access to List Data

To succeed as a real estate investor, you must access a detailed listing data. There are numerous ways to access valuable real estate insights without a license.

You can try to connect with an investor-friendly real estate agent who can provide you access to the MLS. It can be difficult to create this real estate networking relationship at first, but it will be rewarding in the long run.

3.   Online Property Finders

You can use online property finders to get the best investment properties.

4.   Real Estate Analytics

Before you buy an investment property, you need to do your research carefully. You can achieve this using real estate analytics. Real estate analytics will simplify your life and allow you to save enough time when it comes to investing in real estate.

In short, it is possible to become a real estate investor without a license.

Chapter 3: Boring Financial Elements

Knowing Your Position

It is important to know how much money you have and the amount you're ready to put into your business. You need to find your business's working capital from your current assets. Learning how to determine the working capital for your business is as simple as mastering a straightforward formula:

Working capital = Current assets − Current liabilities

Finding your exact working capital is a great financial calculation. Understanding this number will reveal insight into your business's short-term liquidity. The higher your working capital, the more financial freedom you have to grow.

Disclosing Who's Driving Your Money

Identifying and tracking the main drivers of your business is a vital tool for generating profits and ensuring your business remains stable. That is why it's essential to determine what they are, if they are measurable and if they can be improved.

A key business driver is something that has a massive effect on the performance of your specific business.

An extensive list of internal and external factors impacts the performance of every small business. The point is to concentrate on a handful of drivers that:

- Can be executed
- Are measurable

- Reflect the performance and progress of your business
- Can be compared to a standard

Sales or revenue is the leading indicator that's easy to follow. Many businesses measure this at least monthly, but many measures it daily or even hourly. However, sales may not be the actual driver for your business. Instead, it might be the number of sales calls you make or your follow-up campaign. These are the drivers that help you increase sales.

How to Save Enough Money Without Forfeiting All Fun

It can be quite difficult to balance your time now and prepare for the future. But with a few small steps, you can make your short-term plans to act in ways that support your long-term plans.

When you consider life, it can appear like you have a long time to concentrate on the savings goals you want to achieve. However, life can seem to pass by in the blink of an eye, so it's essential to remember to have fun with family and friends, too.

In general, the world consists of short-term doers and long-term planners. It is possible to plan ahead and still make the most of the time you have now, but you may experience challenges matching in weight with the things you do with the things you want in the future. The tension between how you live life and how your brain plans your goals can prevent you from meeting your expectations. Not unless you learn how to balance your focus.

- **Decide to Save-Then Do It** -Do whatever works to get you started, and find ways to help you balance your life.
- **Monitor Your Spending** - Keeping track of your spending can help you, in turn, create a budget for saving, and saving money

to fulfill goals has built-in rewards.

- **Change Incentives for the Better** - Find a way to change your incentives to help balance having fun now with saving for the future.

How to Make More Money at Work

Do you want to make more money? Well, here are a couple of ways you can apply to increase the amount of money you earn at work.

- **Request for a Raise** -Don't wait until your boss offers you more money, that may never happen. Get ready and show them your specific achievements.\
- **Request for a Promotion** - If there is a vacancy, be ready to show them you're qualified for it with your resume and achievements related to the new role.
- **Continue Your Education** - Always search for ways to improve your set of skills or learn new ones.
- **Establish Relationships in, and out of Your Department** - This is a great practice in general. If you want to climb the ladder or make more money, you need cheerleaders.
- **Market Yourself** -Opportunities aren't going to search for you or come into your office. You have to step out to find them.
- **Become Indispensable** - Be, honest, helpful, and positive. You will become irreplaceable because your colleagues will want to work with you.
- **Switch Jobs** - Get a new job.
- **Develop Plan B** - If you depend on a given job 100%, and you might accept less than you deserve because you don't want to lose it.

Chapter 4: Getting Your Duck in a Row

Mastering the Market Cycles

Since the crash of real estate in 2007, there has been a massive recovery in most markets. Many experts think real estate is a bubble that will soon emerge. The pundits say that since real estate market cycles last eight years, and this is the ninth year of successive price gains, a correction is overdue. Interest rates have gone higher by 2.25 percent since December 2008, and many still wonder whether the party's over.

When you understand market cycles, you get insights for what to do with the current assets and whether or not to purchase more. Investing can help you optimize profits and avoid failures. Let's dive into the real estate market cycle and learn to determine where a given market lies in the cycle, and the kind of strategies to apply in every phase of the period.

The Four Phases

The real estate market cycle has four phases. First, is an expansion or the stage during which growth happens. Next is the equilibrium or a period of stabilization. The third phase is Decline, where values drop, sometimes a little, sometimes a lot. The last step, then, is absorption or the phase where property values start to bounce back and recovery starts, but growth is still slow.

Let us discuss each of these market cycle phases in detail.

Phase 1: Finding an Expansion Market

Real estate markets in the expansion phase are places experiencing job growth and population rise. Favorable government initiatives, tax incentives, and low-income tax can result in economic benefits.

For example, when there are good conditions in the market, corporations may be willing to move to or expand in a market. Infrastructure growth and factory expansion bring jobs. More jobs result in population growth, which leads to more building permits, new schools, roads, and shopping centers.

During the expansion stage, great places near downtown and areas with older homes with historical significance can identify renovation and gentrification. Housing inventory can become tight. There will be more buyers than sellers, and sellers will come across numerous offers, with prices always growing higher than list prices. An inventory doesn't remain on the market for a very long period during expansion. Usually, properties sell in days or even hours. Prices rise during development, and appreciation is high.

Actions to Make During Expansion

The early period of expansion phase is the time to build new homes and to generate money doing flips. During the latter period of development, it is good to sell or preferably exchange properties that were bought low during absorption or decline. Then with that cash in hand, buy in other markets that have better cash flow and more room for prices to increase.

Phase 2: Finding a Market in Equilibrium

In the early periods of the equilibrium phase, new inventory hits the market as individuals' sense that things are slowing down and strive to cash out. There are fewer buyers because company expansion and job growth have reduced by the time equilibrium happens. Real estate listings start to sit on the market for 120 days or longer. Prices begin to drop, and sellers pay more concessions because the market begins to favor buyers instead of sellers. During equilibrium, builders offer rewards and start to lower prices. New shopping centers have vacancies, and apartment complexes start to provide incentives.

Actions to Take During Equilibrium

Don't be greedy. If you want to sell and you have good equity, this is the time to make that sell. You may have to sell 10 percent below market value to make sure you get out before the flood of people who will drive the market into decline. For those who want to increase their holdings, equilibrium is the time to purchase-off market properties from distressed sellers where you can still attain pricing that makes sense.

Phase 3: Determining a Market Decline

One of the surest approaches to identify a declining market is to study employment trends. In decline, unemployment increases, jobs are difficult to find; companies limit their workforces. Schools may even allow teachers to go because people relocate from the city to other markets. Signs of decline eventually become clear. Offers are quite low, and there is room for negotiation. Local governments may try to jump-start the market by establishing improvement zones and other development incentives.

Actions to Make During a Decline

If you sold in an earlier market phase and didn't reinvest in a different market, you might have cash in hand. If so, the decline is the period to purchase steeply discounted properties, primarily A and B+ assets. Higher class properties will increase in value the most when the bounce happens, and decline is the perfect time to get these gems for prices that will result in cash flow during a down market. You might also want to identify apartment complexes during a decline. Just be sure that you have sufficient rental demand and that population loss is not.

Phase 4: Choosing an Absorption Market

Absorption starts as prices stop declining. The rise becomes apparent to many investors only when foreclosure inventory starts to become competitive. Absorption may experience the return of multiple offers as a significant REITs, and hedge funds begin to compete for inventory. Prices rise as market conditions start to favor sellers once again. Absorption causes jobs to return and unemployment easing. A great way to consider absorption is though it was the early springtime. There could be snow on the ground, but it is melting, temperatures are warming, but it's still early for shorts and sandals.

Actions to Take During Absorption
Absorption is the period to purchase cash flow properties as you can. Stick to the best neighborhoods. If you increase your portfolio during absorption, you will always cash flow well and receive a bump from appreciation later during the expansion stage.

Remember that all real estate is local and that usually there are markets in each of the four phases of the market cycle somewhere across the country.

Overcoming Real Estate Investment Fears

With real estate investing, many investors, and especially those who are starting, have to deal with anxiety on some level. It might present itself as a reluctance to proceed on a deal, or it might be a full-fledged terror if you find yourself in a financial bind that could have severe and lasting effects.

One of the rubrics to success in real estate is learning how to control fear and overcome it to become a sure-footed, brave investor. So, how can you beat it?

1. **Become Educated**

Most of the fear emerges from the unknown and competition. Maybe your anxiety is saying you don't know much about something. That's OK. Just learn about it. Register for that real estate investing course, read real estate books, do research, and make calculated moves.

2. **Be Ready to Be Helped**

Successful real estate investors and business leaders know that help is essential to their success. Support isn't a sign of weakness. No one knows everything about everything. Embrace help, get coaching, consult mentors, network, and listen.

3. **Take It like a Pro**

Accept the presence of worry, then face it, take advantage of your knowledge, and involve your network to reduce risk and make the best moves you can.

Building Your Real Estate Team

Some real estate agents prefer working on their own for the rest of their careers. Others prefer joining a real estate team than taking on the responsibility of building and managing one.

But if you have decided that you are at a stage where you need to assemble your team, and you're ready to manage one, then you need to know where to begin and what steps to take to succeed.

This section will help you learn how to create a real estate team that is sure to expand your business.

In general, there are several steps you have to complete before you can begin the hiring process. Be sure that if you skip these and start interviewing real estate agents, you're preparing your team up for failure.

Step One: Is It Time for You to Assemble a Real Estate Team?

You might have decided to establish a real estate team, but is it a great decision? This first step reflects where you are in your real estate career.

It's generally agreed that if a real estate agent is managing every side of a transaction, he/she is restricted to 50-60 per year. This implies any more leads that get on the table have to be sacrificed. When you begin sacrificing leads because you don't have the time to control them or provide them with the best services, then it's time to think about creating a real estate team.

On the other hand, if you haven't really agreed on any form of maximum terms of how many real estate transactions you can deal personally, then a team might not be the right channel for you just yet. Instead, you need to concentrate on working on your personal real estate agent career because building a team is not a great solution. Even if a team can help you generate more leads, they first require leads to work with. And you need to be making enough leads where dividing commission on them will not be a big deal. Overall, a real estate team is meant to take your business to the next step, not save it.

So, keep in mind that a successful real estate team starts with a great real estate agent.

Even if you have a decent amount of leads, you want to ensure that you'll always have enough ready for your team. That is the reason some brokers select the option of buying real estate leads.

Step Two: Analyze Your Finances

A considerable advantage of a real estate team is that it will let your business to generate more money. But there is also a rise in expenses. Since you have experience working in your real estate market, with some analysis, you need to determine the costs and budget required.

What are the costs of a general transaction? How many do you think you'll really be handling with every new member of your real estate team? Analyze your finances carefully and ensure you have a 6-month cash reserve to cover your business and personal expenses. This is a measure you take in case you hit a negative cash flow with your team at first.

Ensure you have a solid financial plan in place. A significant problem many real estate teams run into isn't having enough funding to maintain. This can be addressed with some planning.

Step Three: Make Sure All the Relevant Systems Are in Place

As a solo real estate agent, you're generating sufficient leads to establish a team, and you have the finances to hit the ground running. But since this real estate team will depend on you and your business foundations, you have to confirm all the relevant systems are in place and ready for action when the team is presented. Most of these systems are likely in order as you are succeeding in your real estate agent career. However, make sure you review them and confirm that everything is a full-proof and scalable as possible.

Step Four: Agree on the Type of Commission Split

While there are different methods to handle a commission split for your business, the two most common ways include:

- **Graduated Commission Split:** This real estate team plan for commission requires that an agent's commission may be shared out 50/50 at the start. However, as they near specific goals set by the real estate team leader, the commission will be increased to maybe 60/40 and so forth. This generates a form of incentive for team members to fulfill specific goals required to grow the real estate business.

- **100% Commission Split:** This plan for commission implies that each real estate agent on the team earns 100% commission on their lead conversions.

If you are wondering which path you should take, start with the graduated commission split. As the team grows and achieves specific revenue goals, you may decide to shift to a 100% commission split.

Some Tips for Setting Your Commission Plan

- Whatever plan you decide on, keep everything simple. Make sure every team member knows why and how they generate money and how they can generate more.
- Make sure that you're factoring your profit margin first.
- It's a good thing for a commission plan to be fair and based on the amount of work.

Step Five: Develop a Real Estate Team Agreement

Every team member that you add will need to know what's expected of them exactly, their role on the team, and even your position as the team leader. This is the reason why you need to take the time to create a clear draft and detailed team contracts before you start hiring real estate agents. There are templates online that you can use to get started in drafting your own. A basic real estate team agreement should comprise the following:

- A summary of what's expected in terms of performance from the team member.
- A comprehensive compensation plan including how /when the member will receive compensation.
- Specific duties and responsibilities.
- What is under the property of the real estate team leader. Acts as protection in case of departure.
- Employment status.

Step Six: Choose a Real Estate Team Name

This is the last step in getting ready your real estate business for expanding into a team. Choose a team name that you believe will attract clients. Decide on what will make for the best real estate team name and ensure to secure a website and social media pages under this name.

Employing Team Members

Well, at this point, everything is ready for the start of a successful real estate team. Now is the time to look for individuals who will help drive your business. Remember that there is a right time to recruit each one of these positions, and that's only when the demand needs it.

Step 1: Develop a Hiring Process

You don't want to jump into recruiting just any real estate agent. Even if they have a solid record of generating leads and converting them, that doesn't always imply they will be perfect for your team's culture. That's the reason many team leaders depend on various personality tests and traits along with a record of work to decide who to hire.

Besides selecting the approach for who will be recruited, you also want to consider the procedure they'll go through. Will you be interviewing them alone, or as the team grows, will other members talk them too? Will there be separate stages of the interview? Will the process be a long one or a short one?

Keep in mind; it's better not to rush recruiting any member. Hiring a wrong person can cost you, your team, and a lot of time. Of course, there are moments when you strive to do everything right as the team leader and still end up with the wrong individuals. In such a case, the best thing is to hire fast. Don't allow a bad hire to slow down your real estate team for too long.

Step 2: Employ a Real Estate Administrative Assistant

Who should be employed first on a real estate team is one of the things that is most argued about. Experienced real estate agents recommend you hire a buyer's agent first. That's because a buyer's agent is always paid on a 50/50 commission split and not on a salary. And the way these professionals say is that this real estate agent will let you convert leads and finally generate more leads, so you'll be dividing commissions you couldn't be making without them anyway.

But hiring a real estate helper first is a great move. For one, they can be brought on early to make sure the real estate team leader receives support in getting ready all the initial steps in the "Getting Started" section above. Besides that, many real estate teams discover they experience massive turnover with the buyer's agents. These teams are mainly the ones without a supportive admin system in place. For example, the admin will be accountable for carrying contracts to closing, freeing the buyer's agent from the paperwork, and even providing the agent more time to close on more real estate deals.

Also, because you want your real estate assistant to take on most of your daily tasks, freeing you up for lead generation, this person should have a license. This will ensure more tasks delegated to the assistant.

If you're concerned about having to pay for this position's salary, you may not be at the right stage for creating a real estate team.

Step 3: Employ a Buyer's Agent

With the help of your admin support system, you'll manage to generate more leads than before. That's when it's time to take the next step and employ the next person of your real estate team: the buyer's agent. All those leads you had to pass up on before will shift to the buyer's agent. This agent's primary responsibilities will involve lead conversion, display properties, and taking care of any/all buyer's needs, presenting offers, and prospecting for both seller and buyer leads.

Although it might be tempting to recruit a new agent who you can train to perform things your way, it is realistic to go with an experienced real estate agent. With all the systems in place and the admin support, an experienced buyer's agent will manage to handle the expected goal of leads set by the team leader. Don't forget that a successful real estate team starts with a great real estate agent.

Step 4: Employ an Inside Sales Agent

Since you and the buyer's agent will be generating leads, finally, there will come a time when your plates are full, and you will want to introduce your next hire: the inside sales agent. This agent is accountable for generating new leads, handling inbound leads from sign calls and other sources, plus lead conversion.

There are three categories of inside sales agents:

- **Outbound**: In this role, the agent is accountable for generating leads from FSBOs, expired listings, just sold, geographic farms, etc. The agent, in this case, has to be familiar, making cold calls.

- **Inbound/Outbound:** An inside sales agent sometimes picks on the mix of both roles listed above.

Initially, it might appear sensible to hire one inside sales agent to take on both duties. As your team expands, you can split the tasks between two inside sales agents.

Step 5: Employ a Listing Agent

As the lead agent on your team, one of your primary responsibilities will be to take care of listings. However, even with the rest of the members performing other roles, there will come a time where you have all the listings you can handle. That's when it's time to employ a listing agent.

At this point, you will have all the major roles filled on your real estate team. Finally, as your business expands, you might choose to recruit more buyer's agents inside sales agent. You can also factor other duties like a marketing director, personal assistants, and transaction coordinator.

Managing Your Team

At this stage, your team has everything it needs to succeed, but it will all depend on your potential to be a great leader. Although this could be your first time in this position, it is essential to do your best to deliver a support system and help your team. Communicate and interact with each member of the team. Find methods to motivate everyone, be sure to monitor the progress of each agent, and compliment where it's due. Don't fear to delegate-after all, that is the reason you have developed your real estate team.

And remember, you will always need to remain on top of providing leads for your team.

Should I Have a Partner or Do It Myself

Investing with a partner in real estate, more so residential properties, can always be attractive as a business venture because of the many benefits like shared responsibilities.

Entering a real estate investment partnership is a powerful means of real estate investing for beginners, but not only for beginners. Most top real estate investors find beginning a real estate investment partnership to be a highly successful opportunity for purchasing an investment property and optimizing the returns while reducing the costs.

While partnerships can be exciting, you need to proceed with caution. Real estate investment partnerships are like getting started in any other business and should be treated as such. This is even more essential to consider when partnering with family or friends.

Before you decide to partner, ask yourself, "Why am I doing this?" There should be an easily selected, significant benefit to investing with a partner versus investing on your own. It could be any number of items, but if you cannot highlight what it is, probably a partner isn't perfect for the specific opportunity you have in mind.

Although some partnerships are established based on convenience and relationship, a partnership created on necessity and practicality has a considerable probability for success. Most partnerships should have some form of financial or operational consideration as a driving element behind their formation.

Financial Considerations

When it comes to real estate investing, financial constraints are often the single most significant obstacle to overcome. There are a lot of opportunities in the market, but not enough individuals to fund them. Should you allow a great chance to go that way simply because you don't have enough money? Chances are if the odds are good as you think, then the prospective partners might be readily available.

Still, in cases where an investor has the required capital to fund investment on their own, partnerships can eliminate the risk of using all your money.

In summary, doing it yourself may not be the best move, especially when you aren't financially capable.

Real Estate Investment Mentors

Real estate investing can be very frustrating, especially for new investors. There are so many things that you need to learn, and so many questions you need to find answers. Where do you begin searching for a rental property? What kind of investment property matches your financial needs?

It is easy to get lost between a myriad of choices to make, and you're not even sure which decision is suitable. That is why real estate investors are advised to have the right mentor by their side to direct them along the way. For decades, people have been investing in real estate, and if you're offered an opportunity to learn from someone who has achieved what you dream of accomplishing, don't doubt the idea of having a real estate investment mentor.

It's only evident for inexperienced real estate investors to think about how to identify the best real estate investment mentor. Regardless of how experienced we are in a given field, we always look for more ways to gain some little extra knowledge. Attaining more knowledge and looking from a different angle helps us to eclipse our success to the highest limit. Even the current productive investors are never comfortable with their existing knowledge of the housing market and are continually searching for means to learn more.

Getting a real estate investment mentor is likely to help you achieve your goals as a real estate investor. A mentor should be a person that can teach you the best and most professional means to get things done. That takes us to the question of who is defined as a real estate mentor?

Well, a real estate mentor is an individual who works with you one-on-one to close deals on investment properties. They share with you their experience, expertise, knowledge, and the different approaches they use. They offer you advice on real estate investing from their experiences. So, it's pretty obvious having an individual who guides you and helps you out, particularly if you're new in the industry.

But don't think that a real estate investment mentor will do the task for you. They are only there to advise you, and it's up to you to implement the actual work. Some think a mentor should be a guide who assists you when stuck, and others want a mentor to perform all the work for them. There are still those who think a mentor will tell them precisely what to do at all times, and when they don't get that, they give up. So, don't get confused between what a mentor's task is and what your role is. Get a real estate investment mentor who will meet your specific needs.

How to Identify the Best Real Estate Investing Mentor?

There are specific steps you will need to complete to identify a real estate investment mentor who will drive your career to the next level.

1. You want first to establish what it is you want and hope to

accomplish.

2. Then you need to confirm whether or not your vision has requirements to fulfill your goals.

3. You also need to be sure of the amount of risk you are ready to handle because real estate investing can be risky.

4. When you search for your real estate investment mentor, you want to ensure you find an individual who is respectful of you as you are to them.

5. Lastly, you and your real estate investing mentor should have the same goal in mind. Your goals should be one.

Four Questions You Should Ask Before You Select a Real Estate Mentor?

1. What skills does someone need to attain peak performance in real estate?

This is a critical question because it will determine the mentor's knowledge of real estate sales. Their response should touch on real estate sales, such as different approaches to use, how to control revenue and expenses. In case they give an unrelated answer to the question asked, then you can tell that they are not experienced enough to be your real estate investment mentor.

2. What resources are available that will ensure my growth and success?

Depending on your real estate mentor and the advice they offer isn't the answer to improving your skills. Your mentor should suggest your seminars, workshops, websites, and different professional opportunities. These resources should help you enhance your skills and independently succeed in real estate.

3. What experiences have helped you create the desired skills to

succeed?

You should request your real estate mentor what experiences he/she went through that allowed them to succeed and the problems they experienced. Listening to their own experienced will allow you to learn from their mistakes. Find out from your mentor what successes did they most enjoy and what failures they went through. This kind of question will create a closer bond between you and your mentor.

4. What are your goals, and how do you plan to approach them?

In case your real estate investor can provide a clear response and thought-out structure for his / her goals, then you've found the best real estate investment mentor. You need to hear out their goals and their plan to accomplish them because that is the same strategy you need to kick start your career.

The Bottom Line

Having a real estate investment mentor by your side is vital for every investor starting in real estate investing. You can get lost between all the cans and cant's and what-ifs in real estate, but when you have an experienced, successful mentor, you will double your chances of succeeding. A mentor is a powerful way to help you learn from other people's mistakes and rise above the crowd.

Real Estate Networking

Whether you're new to the real estate sector or you're an experienced agent, you probably know the need for real estate networking. Meeting new faces and discussing your business to others is not only crucial for a successful lead generation approach, but also for getting referrals. After all, real estate is a people business. As such, learning how to network correctly is vital for every real estate agent.

Here are some tips about real estate networking.

Where to Network

Anywhere that unites different members of the industry or prospective clients can be seen as a chance for real estate networking. Local charity events, industry conferences, membership group meetings, and industry conferences can create relevant opportunities for real estate agents to get the most out of their time, generally with thousands of prospective contacts gathering in a single place.

If participants have paid to attend a networking event, it's even better. This is because people who pay to take part in a real estate agent network are more serious and more likely to be open to speaking with other industry members.

Additionally, you might want to establish your own events or host a seminar. Though they can require a lot of planning, they're generally worth your time and efforts as individuals will be preparing to speak with you after the event if you do it well.

Keep in mind that real estate networking is about interaction. Therefore, try to take part in a conversation with as many individuals as possible and exchange business cards with those that you speak with. Besides, treat these events as opportunities to learn about new market information and innovations your colleagues are using.

Real Estate Networking with the Right Individuals

The most crucial tip for real estate agents is to network with a different group of people in the industry-not just other agents and prospective clients. A real estate agent network that involves competent and trustworthy people is essential to the success of your real estate agent career.

Apart from experts with whom you work and collaborate with, it's good also to establish relationships and connections with individuals and firms in your community with whom you don't compete. For example, include contractors, real estate attorneys, lenders, and developers to your network. Say your client isn't conversant with the mortgage lending process. If you have an honest lender in your system, you can connect him/her with your client. This ensures you close deals quickly and provides you with a reputation as a hot real estate agent.

Real Estate Networking Online

While personal interactions are the best for creating a real estate agent network, social media is also a great tool to establish connections. Successful real estate agents use social apps such as Twitter, Facebook, and LinkedIn to collaborate with other users, share content that people can interact with, and promote their properties in an easily shareable format. When you're interacting with other people's content, you have the opportunity to know them and establish stronger bonds for when you meet them in person.

Real estate agents should also take advantage of the current and prospective clients they have met by requesting to follow them on social networks. Once connected, it is good to follow up-like some of their photos, comment on their posts, and reach out to them through email or message them via social media platform, and request for an in-person meeting. Although real estate networking online has its advantages, a face-to-face meeting is crucial if you want to close a deal fast.

Master the Techniques of Listening

Becoming a successful agent doesn't imply you have to do all the talking. In fact, listening is an excellent skill for any real estate agent to win more sales. Whether you're speaking to buyers or you're at a real estate networking event, failing to listen to means you're missing out on valuable knowledge that is critical to the people you're communicating with.

Also, most people think the goal of a real estate agent network is to get as many referrals or gather as many phone numbers as possible. However, that can make you desperate. Instead, you should purpose to help and build meaningful business relationships, provide referrals instead of asking for referrals.

Additionally, you can be a more successful real estate agent when you request people for their business cards, instead of giving them yours. This provides you with the chance to contact them and continue to create a connection. But, if your target is to give out as many cards as possible, you may end up waiting for calls that might never come.

The bottom line is that real estate networking is excellent for your agent career. It's an essential factor in your sales success and is one of the best methods to get ahead and establish a long-lasting relationship. It also helps you to learn from members in the industry and boost your profile and approaches to generate leads and close more deals.

Entities

Real estate investing is a business. Although individual real estate investors may not feel like they belong to the company, they typically are. Like in any other industry, real estate business can be classified under separate structures.

Real estate businesses identify these structures not only to fit their business needs but for the benefits. The most common plan for a real estate business is the real estate limited liability company. The title alone is enough to convince real estate investors to get on board, but it is crucial to understand the main advantages and disadvantages of a real estate limited liability company (LLC) to know whether it is perfect for real estate business.

LLC

When real estate investors create a real estate limited liability company, it becomes its own legal entity. In other words, real estate LLC can have its own bank account, have its own tax ID number, and conduct real estate investing business all under its own name. A real estate LLC is liable then for all its own "actions."

Pros of an LLC
- Protect personal assets
- Tax benefits
- Decreased liability for a property owner
- No strict guidelines

Cons of LLC
- Extra charges for establishing an LLC
- LLC is dissolved with bankruptcy

S Corps

S Corporations are much simpler than C Corporations, and thus cheaper to operate. They are less flexible compared to LLCs, but have one main advantage: dividends are excluded from social security taxation if the S Corporation owners are paid a reasonable amount.

Chapter 5: Real Estate Investment Markets

Learning how to research real estate markets is an important skill.

Raw land

Investing in raw land is a solid investment because the supply is limited-nobody is producing any more. While the growth of the population tends to guarantee that land prices will rise, making it an excellent investment, you need to be careful and follow a procedure for your land purchases. Land may also act as a great individual retirement account investment.

Raw land is one of the best investments available. It will always be worth it, and there is a little chance of anyone stealing. Raw land is undeveloped property without any buildings or another structures-it's still in its natural state. If you are thinking about investing in it, the tactic isn't about buying at a high price but selling at the best time for a great price.

Investing in raw land is for individuals who can afford to wait for years until a person comes calling for the property. It's not a great idea for people who want to perform a quick flip or want to generate an instant income stream.

In general, raw land is a significant long-term investment.

Property Location

The value of raw land increases at a faster rate at the center of a developing city, or around the perimeter of cities. However, any raw land in a given place disclosing the growth of the population is worth investment consideration because this growth attracts developers. The whole notion of investing in raw land is to select the property that will increase in value and attract a buyer who will pay more for it down the road.

Raw Land or Developed Property?

Investing in raw land is less costly than purchasing developed real estate in the same area because there are developments on raw land. But banks are somehow cautious about releasing money for raw land that is not being used for any income-generating purpose and will always demand a higher down payment-sometimes 50 percent of the land purchase.

Single-Family Houses

Nowadays, everyone discusses single-family homes-also known as single-family detached homes or detached houses-and how they can be the best real estate investments. Many real estate investors have gone for them compared to other types of investment properties because they can generate higher cash flow, create vast amounts of wealth, and generate a higher profit on investment.

In 2020, the single-family rental market will be excellent. The demand for single-family rental properties is increasing, with more and more people opting to rent properties instead of owning them. The US homeownership rate has, in fact, been on the decline since 2005. This makes the right time for single-family home investing.

However, some beginner real estate investors assume that any detached house makes for a great real estate deal. What they are failing to understand instead is that several factors must be considered to guarantee a successful single-family home investment. Therefore, first-time investors are vital to consider these factors before you can invest in single-family homes.

Location

Like any other investment property, the most critical factor you need to consider before you dive into single-family homes for sale is the location. Tenants will search their home based on location, thus investing in a wrong location can be a costly mistake.

Single-family homes are rented out to families with children; thus, you need to ensure that the home you want to invest in is located in a place that meets all the needs of a family. Tenants with children would want to live in a safe place, an area that has excellent schools, and that isn't far from health centers, shopping centers, and recreational spaces.

Before you invest in single-family homes, you must also ensure to search for areas that are landlord-and investor-friendly. It's also important to mention that the best places for investing in single-family homes are places where investment property taxes aren't quite high and the investment property insurance good. Another thing to consider is that if you ever decide to list your investment property on short-term rental platforms such as Airbnb, ensure to look for locations where it is legal to operate this kind of rental.

Profitability

In real estate investing, you want to generate money by investing in positive cash flow properties. A real estate investment is considered successful when it makes positive returns. This is realized when your income exceeds your expenses, i.e., when you generate profit.

By choosing to invest in single-family homes, an investor acquires high cash flow. The returns obtained from investing in single-family rentals tend to be higher than other rental properties types such as apartments and multi-family homes. The primary reason for this is that tenants are often the ones in charge of all the utility payments in detached properties. This isn't the situation for all other rental properties, where the landlord pays the water, sometimes even the gas and electricity bills. Besides that, single-family homes usually have lower property taxes and insurance rates because they only count as a single dwelling unit. That said, if you are investing in single-family homes, you have a smaller amount of expenses to handle, therefore, enjoy a higher return on investment.

But to ensure that your property will enjoy positive cash flow, it's good that you conduct an investment property analysis before investing in a single-family home.

Buying Price

The main concern for real estate investors is money. When looking for an investment property, the first thing an investor will check is the price to determine whether they can afford to purchase it. Most people opt to invest in single-family homes because they are cheaper than other investment properties. Because of their smaller size, the prices for single-family homes are always set at lower prices regardless of factors such as area, age, and maintenance. This makes them a hot deal to many investors, especially first-time investors who want to purchase their first investment property. And because single-family homes are cheaper, they are easier to buy. In fact, you can acquire a loan from the bank more easily when you make this type of purchase.

Therefore, if you are new to the real estate game, then investing in single-family homes may be the best option for you. But it is good you research all the different investment property financing approaches so you can choose the one that suits you best.

Appreciation of Property

One of the advantages of investing in real estate is the ability to generate money through appreciation. Many investors decide to purchase a real estate property to sell it at a higher price point in the future.

For most real estate investors, single-family homes are the best investment property type. When you compare resale values, it seems like single-family detached homes tend to increase more than other forms of real estate properties. In fact, they see more demand, and this results in high appreciation rates.

For this reason, investors need to search for single-family homes that are found in places recording an economic boom, where the population is rising, business is doing well, development projects are organized, while land and housing are becoming scarce. If you consider all these factors, you are guaranteed to gain from massive real estate appreciation when investing in single-family homes.

Tenants

Tenants play an important factor in the success of a real estate investment. The dream of every real estate investor is to identify good tenants who pay rent on time and cause little problems or none at all.

The great news for those investing in single-family homes is that they have a high probability of working with low-risk tenants. Tenants who decide to live in single-family homes are more stable and responsible than those living in an apartment. This is because people renting a single-family home tend to stay for a longer time, and as a result, you won't have to deal with turnover, vacant rooms, or numerous viewings for potential tenants. They are also likely to take good care of the property as they will handle it as their own home. You can then expect less damage done to your property.

For that reason, investing in single-family homes can provide you with both reliability and stability, and can quickly help you fulfill your investment goals in the long term.

But anything is possible; you can't always be sure that your single-family home renter will be a good one. That is the reason you need to confirm you are getting the best tenant. It is critical to review every prospective tenant thoroughly. Run a credit and background screening to verify that your renter can afford the rental property and that they do not engage in any criminal activity. It's also a good move to contact their employer to verify their employment and call their previous landlords to find out whether they have paid all the rent. You can still hire a rental property management company to do all the work for you, but know that this comes with some fees. Whichever way, the right screening will ensure that you avoid a lot of problems when investing in single-family homes.

Amenities

The physical appearance and property features are essential to attracting tenants. When people search for a property to rent, they make their decision depending on the amenities that the property provides, such as the number of bathrooms, parking spots, and bedrooms, etc.

As said earlier, many single-family homes are rented out to families on a long-term basis. Their primary advantage is that they provide more privacy than any other type of property. Families can feel some sense of freedom and don't have to worry about their upstairs neighbors, especially if they have children who make noise all the time. Besides that, single-family homes almost always have a yard where children can play. If you can get a property with a garden or a play structure, that's even better because it makes the property even more attractive to families.

Therefore, before you buy a single-family home, you must make sure to identify one that has a good number of amenities. Keep in mind that people looking into single-family homes for rent will measure by the properties' physical features. The more facilities you have, the better. This way, you can charge your tenants higher.

In summary, single-family homes have many advantages that make them stand out as the best investment properties. But real estate investors must consider all the factors listed above before making any move to optimize their chances of securing a great real estate deal.

Small Multi-Family

This includes duplexes, triplexes, and quadruplexes. Single-family homes are created for one family, but small multi-family homes are developed for: multiple, smaller families. Typically, it involves 2-4 "sets" of 2bedroom/2bathroom family homes that are all linked to each other as a single building with different walls and doors for privacy. Investors who prefer this kind of real estate typically buy or build these small multi-family properties and rent out every unit to a different family. For instance, the owner of a duplex will have two separate "families" or tenants living in the building. Each family will pay the owner a monthly rent.

Another way investors generate money from small multi-family homes is to "house hack" or live in one side and rent out the other part. For instance, if a real estate investor just bought a triplex (3-unit multi-family home), he or she may decide to live in one of the units and rent out the other two units. Many investors prefer this method because it helps them buy a property to live in and invest simultaneously. Plus, small multifamily investing allows them to gather a vast amount of total rent money without the need to buy multiple homes.

Large Multi-Family Homes

This includes multi-family homes bigger than four units, but usually, this is just the fancy term for "apartment buildings." Apartment buildings aren't nearly as challenging to invest in as people may think. While it is unlikely that you will have the time or money to buy a whole apartment building on your own, in most cases, people invest with others. In fact, most apartment buildings are owned by a group of individuals. When people choose to put their money together to invest in an apartment as a group, we usually refer that a "real estate syndication."

In real estate syndications, you have general partners and limited partners. The general partners work as "active investors," and they are people who look for potential apartment buildings to buy, evaluate the properties, and secure the financing from the bank. The limited partners work as "passive investors," and they are the individuals who put some of their money into the deal and leave all the details up to the general partners.

Overall, the general partners and limited partners invest in apartment buildings and tend to earn a lot of profit. The details of real estate syndications can be a little complex, but typically investors generate money by buying undervalued apartment buildings. Next, they increase the value of these apartments by improving them and increasing the monthly rent. After several years, investors will either sell the building for a higher price or refinance it with the bank. Either way, investors generate profit.

Commercial Buildings

This type of real estate refers to strip malls, warehouses, or commercial premises. Investors buy these buildings or build them, and then rent them out to companies or business owners who require space. It is the same as renting out a house. Instead of your tenants being familiar people who want the area to live in, your tenants are business owners who want the space to sell products to consumers.

The lease that tenants sign to rent space in these buildings is for a more extended time, and the business owner handles typically most of the maintenance issues and repairs himself or herself every time the toilet clog. Therefore, owning these buildings provide you with enough confidence that you will receive your monthly rent always and requires less hassle.

The drawback is that these buildings are expensive to buy. Unlike apartment buildings, there aren't many syndications available. Investors usually buy the building on their own, or with few partners, which might cost them hundreds of thousands of dollars.

Mobile Homes and Mobile Home Parks

When we discuss real estate investing, mobile homes, and mobile homes, parks are not the first things that hit the mind. That's why it is essential to explain what they are before proceeding to discuss how to invest in them.

A mobile home is a type of housing made up of prefabricated structure, developed on a permanently connected chassis, which is then transported to a site. A mobile home can be built on a given place forever or semi-permanently or can also be moved around. Although mobile homes may have many disadvantages compared to standard homes, their most significant advantage is that they are quite cheap. Mobile homes can still be used as a permanent home, vacation home, or as a rental property. Buying and managing a mobile home as an income property has many ups and downs.

On the other hand, a mobile home park is a permanent area for mobile homes. They provide the best opportunities for less wealthy individuals and households for people who move out often.

Why Mobile Homes and Mobile Home Parks Among the Best in the Us Market?

Despite individual negative perceptions, mobile homes and mobile home parks have gained a lot of popularity in the US in the past few decades. This is true both in terms of housing and real estate investing. But why would so many people prefer to live in a prefabricated permanently attached rental property or home? The answer is affordability. Mobile homes cost only a fraction of the price of standard homes, which is a considerable advantage in a community where many people are forced to live on $20k or less per year.

REITs

This is when individuals put a certain amount of cash into a substantial fund to invest with other people. Unlike real estate syndications, the managers of these funds use that cash to invest in different real estate deals, not just a single large deal. These funds are managed through companies, and hence the name real estate investment trusts (REITs).

Through REITs, people invest in more real estate deals than they would have been able to do on their own. Hence, REITs allow investors to diversify their investments and protect them from risk. If a single real estate deal fails to work out, then they can depend on other deals in the fund to secure them from losing money. Most people prefer to invest in real estate using REIT because it is passive. You are not a landlord; you don't need to do repairs or collect rent payments. You only need to put your money into the REIT and allow the manager of the fund to handle all the details.

In conclusion, these are many different types of real estate markets. Your first step as a real estate investor should be to get familiar with each of them so that you can select the best option for you. You can purchase land on which to build or buy it with plans to sell it to a different person. You can concentrate on single-family homes and rent them out, buy them wholesale and sell to someone else for a higher price, or fix and flip them. You can try to rent out small multifamily deals, or decide to concentrate on apartment buildings through real estate syndications. Once you generate a decent amount of cash, you may want to dive into commercial and industrial buildings that you can rent out to other business owners. If you're going to become more passive and invest some of the retirement money you got from your job, REITS might be the best option.

As you can see, there are many ways to invest in real estate. These are just some of the key techniques. All you need to do is to select the one that best fits your lifestyle and goals.

Chapter 6: Real Estate Investment Strategies

Real estate investing provides different property investment strategies that suit the needs of various real estate investors. The right real estate investment strategy for you depends on the amount of money you are ready to invest and time. Most importantly, your long-term real estate investing goals. That is chapter will focus on the different real estate investment strategies that you can use to get started. Keep reading to learn more.

Buy and Hold

If you are getting into real estate for the first time, you're going to want to learn about one of the best strategies in the industry-the buy and hold real estate investment strategy. Let's explore the details of this long-term investment strategy.

Buy and hold is one of the most popular investment strategies, and it's widely considered as the best method to diversify any investment portfolio. The buy and hold real estate investment strategy is precise as the name says; it is a means of buying an investment property to hold it for a given period of time-usually five years or more. So, you're not buying, flipping, and instantly selling an investment property for a quick profit. Although buy and hold real estate investors may want to sell their investment properties, that is more so down the line.

During the "holding" period, the investment property is defined as a rental. Renting out the property is where the profit on investment comes in. If the buy and hold real estate investment strategy is done properly, you can earn from short term gains through positive cash flow and long-term real estate appreciation.

The buy and hold real estate investment strategy depends on how you will invest in real estate if you're a beginner. This is because it is one of the most straightforward approaches for first-time investors, as compared to the fix and flip strategy, which demands experience to identify the right distressed properties. It's also a favored technique among experienced property investors who want to create wealth over time from equity build-up and property appreciation.

Types of Buy and Hold Real Estate

Rental properties exist in different sizes, purposes, and shapes. To ensure you're optimizing your buy and hold real estate investment strategy, you should identify the type of property you want.

Below are different types of income-generating assets you can invest in using the buy and hold real estate investment technique:

Turnkey Real Estate

When you invest in a turnkey real estate, you purchase a move-in ready property, which already has professional property management and also has tenants already living inside. In other words, everything is taken care of. Your role is to "turn the key" and you will get a robust investment property.

Vacation Rental Property

The vacation rental market has been solid of late. If you invest in short term rentals can be an excellent rental strategy if you select the correct market at the right time.

Single-Family Home

This usually is used with the traditional rental technique; you invest in a typical house and rent it out to a tenant. Many beginners select single-family homes as a means to get a feel of the real estate investing industry. One rental unit and one tenant ensure everything is simple.

Multi-Family Home

If you want more, then a multi-family home is the best option for the buy and hold real estate investment strategy. A multi-family property is one with more than one housing unit. They are cheaper than a single-family home, but because you're renting multiple units to multiple tenants, you'll be generating higher rental income. It's the best for steady cash flow and quickly building your investment portfolio.

Commercial Real Estate

The buy and hold real estate investment technique isn't just about residential real estate. Investors can buy a property used for business functions like an office building or retail store. But commercial real estate investing could be more complicated, particularly for beginners.

Pros of Buy and Hold Real Estate Strategy

This strategy comes with various benefits. Besides cash flow, there numerous advantages to investing in buy and hold real estate. Let us see.

1. Rental Income

Why property investors go for this option is the monthly rental income. There might be other sources of generating revenue, such as laundry, vending machines, and parking income. If you have a long-term rental or employ professional property management, all the generated revenue will be passive income, and you can generally account for it on a monthly plan.

2. Tax Deductions

Rental expenses aren't all terrible-most if not all, qualify for a tax deduction. Besides property tax benefits, there is a significant number of costs you can clear, such as depreciation and mortgage interest and loan origination fees. Other operating expenses, such as maintenance and repairs, are tax-deductible.

3.   Equity

Financing investment property is conducted through bank loans. The best thing about the buy and hold real estate investment strategy is the tenants of your rental property end up paying your mortgage. As the rent you collect covers the mortgage payments, the equity in your property increases every month. Tenants will even pay your interest costs. The secret here is to get good tenants.

4.   Appreciation

Real estate appreciation may also be a powerful thing that comes out of the buy and hold real estate investment strategy. Real estate markets can vary over the years, but if you pick a great city to buy and hold, your rental property will gain value with time. In general, buy and hold real estate increases at an annual rate between 3-5 percent.

House Flipping

Flipping houses is one of the short-term real estate investment strategies. Put simply; you buy a property that is selling for a price below the market value. However, the property is always in poor condition and requires renovations. In most cases, the property is still in a distressed state and requires rehabilitation. What you do in this case is to improve the property at your own expenses and then resell it. In this situation, you should ensure that the price for which you are selling is enough to take care of the expenses and the profit margin.

Why Is House Flipping One of the Best Real Estate Investment Strategies?

Massive Profits

Why real estate investors go for a fix and flip is the profit. One of the best things about real estate flips is the opportunity to generate high profits in a short time. This is what makes a fix and flip one of the best short-term real estate investment strategies.

Gaining Experience and Knowledge Faster

Fixing and flipping involve many operations and transactions that a real estate investor would have to handle. However, this is the best way to learn more about real estate investing. Throughout your experience with a real estate fix and flip, you will learn more about expenses, construction, and the local real estate market.

Minimum Competition

One thing about fix and flip real estate is that it is a risky strategy. For that reason, not many real estate investors attempt to risk with such real estate investment strategies. This leaves you with little competition in the real estate market, which implies that you have a higher probability of client turnout.

Fast Appreciation

House flipping is the best investment technique for fast appreciation. Once you buy the property and begin renovating it, it increases in value. This is referred to as forced appreciation. When you finish renovations, the property automatically increases in market value. This means you will ask for a higher price that covers all the renovation costs plus a great profit margin within the deal.

If you are a beginner real estate investor, then it is good to start with low-risk investments first. Fix and flip are one of the high-risk real estate investment strategies. Investing in rental properties would make better sense until you gain the required experience to flip properties.

Wholesaling Real Estate

Real estate wholesaling is another awesome real estate investment strategy. But, to succeed in this technique, you need to master everything about it. Wholesaling real estate applies the same concept as house flipping, and the only difference is that instead of flipping houses, you will flip contracts. In other words, you look for a motivated seller, agree on a below-market sales price before you identify a buyer to sell the buying contract. In this case, you act as a middleman between the buyer and the seller. As the wholesaler, you generate profit once the deal is finished. The advantage is the difference between the contracted price with the seller and the amount paid by your buyer.

Wholesaling is an excellent technique if you want to get your feet wet into real estate but don't have enough cash. An advantage of wholesaling is the time it needs to wholesale, which is shorter than flipping houses. Additionally, you will not incur the costs of making repairs and improvements. As a result, you take on massive, less risk. But the process of wholesaling real estate step by step is also faced with its obstacles. Some of the challenges of wholesaling real estate include confusion about its legality and complicated contracts.

What Is the Perfect Way to Generate Money Through Real Estate Wholesaling?

While real estate wholesaling is a great way to make income in real estate, the amount of money you generate depends a lot on your client base. What this means is that if you decide to wholesale investment properties, it can be a far better choice than regular residential properties. The reason is apparent: there is always a real estate investor out there who wants to buy investment properties. It is easier for you to get an end-buyer who wants to invest in property instead of living in it. Real estate investors are always looking for the best deals in the real estate market, and, in this case, you have what they want. In this case, targeting a specific niche of clients might be a great strategy to go about generating money in real estate.

Turnkey Investing

If you've done any analysis into real estate investing, you've probably heard the term "turnkey real estate." Businesses that refer to themselves as "turnkey companies" promise to manage all the parts of real estate investing-helping you with all features of buying and maintaining a rental property. Leaving you with time to sit back and collect passive your income.

Put simply, turnkey real estate investing is a loosely defined investment technique that the investor buys, rehabs, and has a property controlled through a third-party, generally from a long-distance means. They aim to make the whole real estate investment process as simple as possible, so what you need to do is to "turn the key." Right?

There are many turnkey real estate providers in America and across the globe, and no two companies are precisely the same. Some will purchase, rehab, rent, and then sell a property to you, the investor. Others may help you locate the property and allow you to conduct most of the heavy lifting on the rehab side for you. Again, each company runs its operation differently, so if you choose to go with a turnkey company, it is good that you do some research to find exactly what that turnkey company will and will not do.

Advantages of Turnkey Investing

Since a turnkey property is one that is fully renovated and ready to be purchased, it means that no additional work is required in terms of repairs, and the property can be rented out immediately after buying. Most of the time, these companies will sell you a property that is already "performing," which implies a tenant is already living inside.

Turnkey Companies and Property Management

Many turnkey companies provide property management services. The focus is to polish up everything as much as possible so that an investor can have an easy way of running his property.

Getting a property manager can be a big hassle for many investors, and taking advantage of the turnkey company's property management services is the best way to start. But note that you're not entitled to this property management for the rest of your investment. You can employ another if needed, but they are banking on the notion that they'll do a great job, and you'll not have the drive to seek another one.

The Drawback of Turnkey Companies

Convenience comes with a specific cost.

What turnkey operators charge is different. Some have acquisition fees.

Some own the properties and sell them to you at a slight high charge. Some may own the property management company, and they receive payment through fees.

Whichever way, as the buyer, it is right for you to know what the fees are. Of course, taxes are sometimes the unavoidable cost of running a business.

House Hacking

The term "hack" points to some form of a scheme that falls short of hitting a real goal. That's why you might have ignored this investment strategy until now.

House hacking happens when you purchase a multi-family investment property and live in one of the units. The rental income you collect from other units should facilitate most of your housing expenses.

While the definition may not prove how great this strategy is, but it's an excellent investment strategy for beginners. It could even be one of the best ways to hit the ground running in real estate.

The common reason why you should use house hacking as an investing strategy is that you get to live in your home for free. Besides this, house hacking offers a huge opportunity cost. Every dollar you spend on rent or even paying a mortgage for a home you live in-none of it generates any return on investment. All that time, you're missing out on the cash you could be making had you put those pennies into a cash flow real estate investment. It's a missed chance to generate money.

So, while the concept of living in a house for free is good, house hacking is more than that. It's based on a long-term plan for generating money, financial independence, and perhaps even early retirement. Purchase a property, live for free thanks to rental income, and save those housing funds for a real estate investment that you'll see returns on.

The 3 Steps to Hacking Your House

1. **Analyze Investment Property Financing Choices and Receive Pre-Approval**

Find a rental property mortgage with the least, fixed interest rates, and an affordable down payment.

2. Identify the Best Real Estate Deal

Identify an affordable or below market value investment property. For example, fixer-uppers, foreclosed homes, and homes with "motivated sellers."

3. Conduct Investment Property Analysis

Run a basic investment property analysis to identify a property with enough rental income to cover housing costs.

All this has to take place with any of the following multi-family homes:

- Duplex
- Triplex
- Fourplex

Short-Term (Vacation) Rentals

We are all searching for the best way to generate money, and one of the beauties of real estate investing is the numerous options it provides to make some additional income. However, with unlimited ways to make money in real estate, there are many questions that you have to answer before you can become a successful real estate investor. One of those important questions is whether short-term rentals are the best investment strategy for beginner investors?

Unfortunately, as with many questions in real estate investing, this one doesn't have a straightforward answer. The answer depends on many factors.

That aside, most beginner real estate investors find it easier to purchase a short-term rental property to get started in real estate investing.

This then means vacation rentals are a good investment option for beginners. There are various benefits linked to buying a vacation rental property, particularly for beginner real estate investors.

Here are some reasons why vacation rentals are a good investment option for beginners.

1. More Rental Income

A significant benefit of investing in vacation rentals is that you can generate more rental income as a beginner real estate investor. If you select a great location, vacation homes tend to attract many tourists and travelers during the high season. During these periods, you'll get to charge high rental rates because of the high demand. The rental income you get helps you pay the mortgage and other additional costs related to the property.

2. There Is Room for Mistakes

Owning a vacation home rental is a great way to learn about real estate investing while having some room to make mistakes. Because of the high number of tenant turnover, you can become an expert on property management problems and solve them with the next booking.

3. Dual-Use Property

The notion of having a dual-use property appears very interesting, whether you're a newbie or an experienced one. With a vacation rental, you can use the investment property to spend your own holidays while renting it out for the rest of the year.

4. Real Estate Appreciation

Vacation rentals are usually in demand, which implies that their values are increasing all the time. When the period comes that you choose to sell the investment property, earn the profits you made, and use it to finance another investment property.

5. **Easy to Get Guests**

Applications like Airbnb, VRBO, and HomeAway have made it easy to find guests.

Live-In House Flips

A live-in house flip is where the investor lives in the house, which they intend to flip. Just like any other strategy for investing in real estate, a live-in flip has benefits as well as challenges

Pros

- **One Mortgage** - If the house you want to flip is your primary residence, you will not need to pay a mortgage and carrying the cost.
- **No Pressure for Reselling Quickly** -In the traditional house flip, the house flipper buys a property with the purpose to improve and sell it fast. In this case, if you don't get a buyer quickly can be very disappointing because you are still paying a mortgage and carrying costs. However, if you are living in the property, you don't need to be scared of secondary expenses.
- **Nice equity** - You can decrease costs significantly by performing some of the repairs and renovations when you're on-site flipping properties yourself instead of employing someone.
- **Section 121 exclusion** - If you have lived in your home for more than two years after purchasing it, you will be excluded from paying capital gains tax while selling the property.

Cons

- Longer wait period
- Risk of damaging the on-going work
- Live in the midst of renovation.
- Selling the live-in flip will mean that you search for another place to live.

BRRRR Investing

BRRRR strategy is one of the best techniques to create wealth in real estate investing.

BRRRR is an abbreviation that stands for Buy-Rehab-Rent-Refinance-Repeat. Real estate investors frequently implement this technique numerous times over their careers. It is a unique structure that represents a hybrid between active and passive income. When executed correctly, you can establish a rental property portfolio without consuming all your cash.

Typically, you buy an investment property below market value and fix it up. The rehabbed property is later rented out to tenants to generate rental income that allows you to pay the mortgage, earn returns, and establish equity over time. Once a sizable amount of ownership in the property is created, you finance it to purchase a second investment property, and so forth. If done right, you can collect most of your original capital back out for this deal.

As you can see, the role of the BRRR strategy is to allow real estate investors to earn and build a portfolio of passive income rental properties without the need to save up for a down payment for each investment property. This is not a get-rich-quick scheme, but it's a powerful means to get started in real estate investing and purchase multiple properties when you don't have cash available.

Student Rentals

Student rental investing is lucrative. It's a powerful strategy. Investing in student housing in college towns is the best investment. College towns are one of the best places to invest in real estate. There's a huge demand for rental property. Students usually flock to college towns at the start of the school every year, and they need rental properties to stay in.

Another tip for choosing to invest in student housing is that you know you are expecting high demand. So, there is a good feeling that you gain as an investor. Off-campus housing is an excellent option for students as on-campus housing. Many students, in fact, prefer off-campus housing because it can be more affordable.

There's significant growth in the student housing sector, and properties are selling for a massive sum of cash.

Chapter 7: The Best Methods to Find Great Real Estate Deals

In the fast-growing world of real estate investment, how do you rise above the rest?

How can you stay competitive in real estate investing? Well, it's not easy. In fact, many investors give up along the way, saying the common phrase "I can't find any deals" or "The deals don't make sense right now."

In this chapter, you'll learn two ways to compete and win, no matter the market conditions and the quality of deals present. It narrows down to two simple ideas that will ensure you stay in the game for the extended period:

1. Create a reliable network of trusted deal providers who can offer you with off-market deals.

2. Apply the "LAPS" technique to analyze the deals you get and make firm offers quickly.

It's All Narrows to Your Network of Deal Providers

You need a network of local deal providers (wholesalers, property managers, and brokers) who enjoy working with investors, understand their unique needs, and are ready to take the time to build a trusting, long term connection with you. Once you identify people having this mindset, make sure that they know, like and trust you. Once you represent an opportunity to investors, they will start to present to you the coveted off-market deals that rarely make it to the MLS. These deal providers want to establish that you will close their deal, and they will gain from you long term. If you're analyzing a deal on the MLS, it has most likely been reviewed by multiple investors for different reasons-normally price and repair cost uncertainties.

How do you find people to present you off-market deals? There are many brokers and property managers out there, and a rapid Google search will quickly uncover the key players in your market. Then it's about having meetings to determine whether they are on the same page and ready to work with you to generate deals. To get other real estate professionals, for instance, wholesalers, search your local Real Estate Investor Association meetings. Lastly, online resources and national conferences are the best places to interact and meet national deal providers.

Once You Create the Network, the Next Thing Is Detailed Analysis and SPEED

When an MLS off-market deal becomes available, the essential factors in gaining an edge against competing investors are speed and financing. When a great deal pops up, you quickly spot it. Most importantly, the network of people who generate off-market deals already knows you have financing ready to close on a deal as long as it fulfills the criteria.

Analysis Process: Run "Laps" Around the Competition

Here is what it takes to analyze deals. Imagine a bracketed competition like the actual basketball tournament. If you have 100 deals, which ones beat out the rest during every round of analysis and number crunching? Which makes it to the semi-finals, finals, and finally the championship.

In other words, what processes and systems do you use to choose that one great deal that rises to the top beating hundreds of other deals that appear on your desk each month? How do you quickly filter the deals that don't fit your criteria or financial needs and ensure the one you close on is profitable?

Well, you apply the LAPS system. LAPS stands for Leads, Analysis, Proposal, and Success.

Breaking Down the LAPS System

Leads: In this process, you collect leads for deals from different sources, including MLS aggregators, wholesalers, real estate, etc. These sources already know the criteria and will call or send an email when a new property emerges that you're ready to make an offer.

You can use various "rules of thumb" to determine whether or not a lead is worth further exploration. One of these rules of thumb is location criteria. The property must be a solid B neighborhood, or else it's automatically discarded. Another rule of thumb is the 1% rule; this requires that you target properties where monthly rents are at least 1% of the buying price. For example, if you plan to buy a $100, 000 properties, you need to receive a monthly rental income of $1, 000. In case a property fails to meet this rule, we'll continue analyzing new leads that match this rule.

You'll require relevant deal sources to ensure your deal flow consistently, so make sure you're continually creating your network of industry professionals who understand your approach and provide regular off-market deals.

Analysis

If, in a regular quarter, you analyze 300 deal leads, only 100 or so will fulfill the location and essential investment criteria. From there, you can go further deep into the deal to find out whether it fulfills other investment criteria.

Property analysis is divided into four financial categories:

- Expected Rent-What is the rent you think you can earn for the property.
- True expenses for the Property-These involves Trash, property management, HOA, repairs, and maintenance, and many more. All these factors must be taken care of before you determine your cash flow number.
- Repair Costs-Get the opinion of a professional contractor and building inspector on what the expected repair costs will be to improve the building into a condition where you can charge market rents.
- After repair value- Once you fix up and repair the property and bring it to the market rent, how much would you sell on the market for?

Once you have removed properties that don't meet the 1% rule and finished the initial analysis based on the four financial elements, you subject each remaining deal through four final criteria tests to confirm whether they qualify to make an offer on:

1. Cash Flow-You need to invest in deals that cash flow positively after factoring all deal expenses.
2. Cash on Cash Return on Investment-Deals should earn a minimum of 9% profit on our cash invested in the deal.
3. Equity- Buy properties between 20%-30% below MLS market value.

4. Total Return-This refers to the amount you earn of you hold the property for x years.

Proposal or Offers Presented

Out of the 100 deals you analyze, only 10 may pass the four screening tests required for you to make an offer. So, you should proceed to present offers on all 10 of these deals and find out whether they are accepted.

Success

Now, out of the 10 offers you make, only one gets accepted. As a real estate investor, your offer will always be much lower than those of retail home buyers, so there's a higher chance it will get accepted. However, this is a numbers game, and just like in a game of basketball, the more shots you take, the more often you'll hear the swoosh of a closed deal.

Something More on Timing and Speed

You will push deals through the analysis pipeline as quickly as possible. Once you identify a great deal, you're ready to present an offer. But before you do that, let's discuss something about timing, as this is a crucial factor for gaining a competitive advantage.

When it comes to offering acceptance, you need to be the first or last. But never be in the middle.

What does that mean? If the listing is already on-market, the first offer received is what the seller measures all other offers against, and there is a natural bias toward the first. Therefore, presenting an opening offer that's an investor –grade, defensible, and market favorite, will provide you an edge. If you correctly analyzed the deal using the LAPS technique and sought the suggestion of the deal provider, you can be sure that your offer will be considered.

If you fail to make the first offer because of some reason, then wait for it to sit for a while. This time frame can only be measured by the heat of the market and the price of the property, but only if it has been sitting for 30-90 days, the current price isn't market appropriately. If you get a word from the listing agent that offers have significantly dropped, it's time for you to present an offer to the table. If you time it well, and the seller wants to get it over with, then your offer may be accepted.

Great Tactics for Finding Great Deals

Surf Craigslist

Craigslist is an online classified platform where it's free to post and browse, so it makes a powerful resource for finding real estate deals. You can find deals in Craigslist by Searching for sellers, posting an ad, and search for landlords. Take a look at the property listings on Craigslist in your targeted area if you're looking for a low-investment, low-commitment method for how to locate off-market real estate deals. You can save more time and money by bargaining directly with a seller instead of working with a local real estate agent.

The MLS

MLS is a traditional strategy for house hunting. If you have a property to sell or want a house to buy, the MLS is where your agent turns to. This is the first place most people turn to while looking to purchase real estate.

Drive Around and Search for Telltale Signs That a Seller Is Motivated

Dull siding, tall grass, overgrown landscaping, and a driveway that needs repair are all indicators that a homeowner has checked out. You need to be driving around to look for properties that don't appear very loved. You can always get some of the best deals on properties for sale by getting owners who don't have the motivation or ability to handle their properties any longer. Don't forget to search for vacant properties.

Buy Online Ads Targeting People Who Will Be Selling Soon

People who are close to selling their homes always search for packing materials, rental trucks, moving services, and related things. You can market to individuals who are in the early stages of planning to move using keywords that aren't related to real estate. This might help to plant an idea about selling directly before a prospective seller gets in touch with a real estate agent.

You need to also commit some of your budgets for online ads to target individuals who are behind on property taxes. Most people who have fallen back are just months shy from deciding to sell. There's an excellent chance to get your hands on prime properties because of divorce.

Use Direct Mail to Target Motivated Sellers

Direct mail presents a powerful way to expand your reach and ensure potential sellers know that you are a friendly person. If you want to avoid wasting money, make sure that direct mail is targeted to specific people.

The best group to target may depend on the region where you're looking to hit real estate deals.

Embrace Networking

Business is always about good relationships. As such, one of the best ways to find off-market real estate deals is by networking with people who know a lot about real estate deals. The right networking strategy gives you a head start to off-market properties. There are many people you should include in your inner working circle for your business. For beginners, you should have a connection with other real estate investors.

Train Your Own Wholesalers

Wholesaling is a great tactic to find real estate deals if you don't want to do the hard work. You can find wholesalers, and train them so that they know what they're doing to make sure you're getting the best deal and saving money when purchasing a property.

Get an Edge on Probate Properties

A lawyer can be helpful when it comes to finding properties that are likely to hit the market soon. However, it's not a must to know a lawyer to find probate homes as your real estate deals.

Probate properties are always much cheaper than traditional properties because they are being sold through a court-appointed representative as part of a will.

The easiest way to find these properties is by going to your local probate court and request to speak with the person in charge of probate matters. It's a great thing to ask for records that cover the last six months.

Cautions When Searching for the Best Deals on Properties for Sale

There are some challenges you'll want to avoid as you look around for the best deal real estate investors can locate. You'll generally want to be cautious in matters dealing with competitors and saying too much. It's possible to network while still maintaining your strategies.

It is also vital to ensure you're not marketing to the wrong people. There's nothing wrong with starting with a small, targeted audience when investing money in marketing efforts. Casting a wide net isn't the best step when it comes to finding motivated sellers. The truth is that people who don't want to sell their homes really cannot be convinced. What you're trying to do is deliver a nudge to people already motivated.

You may also want to carry out your due diligence if you choose to seek a foreclosure property. That means looking for any existing claims or liens. You may also want to confirm that a property doesn't have any occupants. Don't allow a failure to follow the right procedures cost you time, money, and legal headaches.

That said, it helps to step out and look at what's happening in the market around you as you search for rock-bottom property deals. But you can still cover a lot of ground online, which will help you with every point outlined above.

Online resources can help you explore background information about a given property.

Chapter 8: Means to Finance Your Real Estate Deals

Real estate is one of the best methods of investing because not only does it generate good returns, but it also protects the investor from inflation. Despite it being a lucrative investment, it requires capital.

Most beginner real estate investors aren't able to fund a real estate deal using their own money. Very few people are lucky enough to have readily available cash to start their real estate careers.

However, the most prevalent misconception about real estate investing is that you need a lot of money to get started. The absence of enough capital for a down payment continues to prevent many first-time investors from getting started. The thing that most people don't know is that there are real estate investment financing methods that work for beginners.

As a first-time investor, understanding how to get started financing your real estate investment is just as important as finding one. The way a given real estate deal is funded can also be determined by its outcome.

Whether you are a beginner or end-user, here are some methods you can use to finance your real estate investment.

Conventional Mortgages

A conventional mortgage is the most popular investment property loan type. To qualify for one, you need to make a particular down payment, and then the bank gives you the rest of the cash. Although conventional mortgages typically have lower interest rates, they adhere to strict guidelines. You need to have enough down payment, good credit score, and a low debt-to-income ratio. These requirements can prevent other investors.

Conventional mortgages are the best for buy-and-hold investors who want to develop a real estate portfolio of income properties. The mortgage repayments are always made monthly, making them easy to budget. One last thing that you should remember about conventional mortgage loans is that they are not used for short-term financing.

Private Money Lenders

Private money lenders are also an excellent investment financing option for beginner investors. They are nonprofessional individuals who give investment property loans at an offered interest rate and payback period. They are always interested in investing in the property just like you.

If you have a good network, you can use capital from your personal system. This could be a friend, co-worker, family member, etc. Private money loans require minimum qualifications than conventional loans and have a more flexible loan structure. These loans are usually acquired by real estate investors who believe they can increase the value of an investment property over a given period through renovations.

Home Equity Loan

Although this method may not work for everyone, it's a powerful way to take advantage of any equity you already have in another property. A home equity line of credit can be used to get capital from a property you already own to buy a new property. The beauty of purchasing an investment property using this financing method is the ability to replicate it endlessly. Real estate investors can allow their investment properties to pay for their own costs.

Owner Financing

In this method, the seller of the real estate property can act as a lender for the real estate property. This happens by providing the buyer with a given payment plan. Next, the property buyer or real estate investor will make monthly payments to the seller until the price of the property is covered.

Owner financing can be a lucrative opportunity for the seller because he or she can charge more for his/her property using an interest fee for the funding.

Partnerships

If you can't cater for investment property financing alone, you can join hands with another person to finance the property. Real estate partners will always divide the profits based on their contributions. Partnerships will allow you to earn your investment property early and can be customized to suit the needs of the partners. If you have the plan of buying an investment property, but you're short of finances, bringing in a partner who can provide the funding while you handle the management can be a great option. You and your partner will create a contract detailing your responsibilities and how the profits will be shared.

Real estate partnerships can be a great way to launch your rental property investment career. A partner can be used to finance the whole investment property or make the down payment. They might have a passive or active role in the investment property, as agreed by both parties in the existing agreement.

Hard Money

Hard money lenders are a great investment property financing approach where the funds for the real estate investments are released by a private business, instead of a bank. It's always based on the value of the investment property. Hard money loans don't have to go through corporate procedures; thus, they still have a looser requirement for approval and can be secured much faster. This allows you to close quickly when you have a great deal on your hands.

Real estate investors typically go for this option on a short-term basis as bridge loans to get the deal before they can secure long-term traditional financing. This can be an excellent way to offer a flip. However, hard money lenders might be open to supporting risky projects.

Also, these loans have a very high-interest rate and short-terms and always require personal collateral or substantial down payment. They have a low loan-to-value ratio compared to other types of financing and need to be used with caution, with a comprehensive exit strategy.

Lease Option

In some situations, investment property financing can happen through the lease option. You can invest in a property by signing a lease agreement by making little payments until you achieve the money to buy it, usually in two or three years. A fraction of the monthly payments is used as a buying price of the property. Renting the property provides you with enough time to find financing, or save up for down payment.

FHA Loans

If you are buying your first investment property, you can use a mortgage approved by the Federal Housing Administration. The FHA loan was started to motivate homeownership. However, you can purchase a multi-family home with a down payment of only 3.5%, select one unit to live in and rent out the rest to qualify. This makes FHA loan cost-effective real estate investment financing method, mainly if it's your first.

Portfolio Loans

Portfolio mortgage lenders can set their own rules for investment property loans. Since you don't know what to expect, you need to be ready to pay more for these. But the advantage is that you might be able to put less down with this kind of loan.

Commercial Loans

These can be somehow expensive and complex to set up. The application process for a traditional commercial real estate loan demands more time and documentation to complete. However, for those of you who are interested in buying properties with more than four units, this is another option. Remember, however, that if your credit score isn't high, or the property requires renovation, you can expect to pay higher investment property mortgage rates.

Investment property financing can be a complicated task for any real estate investor. As you can see, there are many ways to finance an investment property. Successful real estate investors know how to tell the investment property financing option that will be suitable for each deal. To select the best one for your investment, you may have to do extensive research.

Chapter 9: Real Estate Closing Strategies

Closing real estate deals could be the most exciting thing investors experience throughout their careers, but that doesn't imply the process isn't lengthy and a bit confusing. In fact, there is a broad network of new investors that want to close their first deal, but don't know how to. With the right system in place, closing real estate deals isn't a difficult task, but a crucial moment in an investor's career.

Traditional Selling with a Real Estate Agent

If you're a beginner investor, and this is your first time selling a property, the best way to go about it is to hire a real estate agent or realtor. A right agent will direct you through the entire home selling process and increase your chances of a quick sale. Agents will also help in most of the upcoming steps of selling real estate homes like setting a competitive price, marketing, communicating with the buyer's agent, preparing paperwork, negotiating offers, etc.

For helping you with the home sale, a listing agent will charge a 5-6% commission of the sale price of your home, which then is shared with the buyer's agent. This is the reason why some homeowners avoid hiring a real estate agent; instead, they sell their home themselves to save on paying the commission. However, it's wrong advice to try to sell your home on your own, especially if it's your first time.

Besides, the right agent will be more than a make up for the cost and allow you to get the most money for your home. So, don't only hire any agent, but look for one that's a professional and has an excellent record of sales that show they know how to sell your house fast. You

Selling FSBO (For Sale by Owner)

When you sell your home, it's obvious to want to get the most significant return on your investment at the closing table. For that reason, some homeowners prefer selling their homes without a real estate agent. Referred to as a "for sale by owner," or FSBO, selling a house without a real estate agent requires ambition, time, and drive.

An FSBO can result in massive savings when you deduct the usual 6 percent commission fee for a real estate agent. On a $200,000 home, that could add up to $12, 000 in savings.

Homeowners who are speculating how to sell a home by owner should know that it's a learning process. After all, selling a home isn't something that people do every day. Getting ready for what's ahead will allow you to get the most money at closing and reduce your headaches.

Here Are Steps on How to Sell Your Property by Owner

Prepare Your Home for Sale

The first and most crucial step when FSBO of sale homes is preparing the investment property ready for the market. Real estate investors want prospective buyers to love the park. You can do so by fixing and taking care of any significant problems that you might encounter before listing the property on the market for sale. Get your house inspected to help you identify hidden issues that you might not be aware of, which could prevent a deal. Little repairs can create a difference.

These problems can include things such as carpet stains, damage to the yard, and pet damage. But it is good to conduct improvements that add value to the investment property such as new carpets, bathroom remodel, and landscaping. Before you erect the "For Sale" sign out, clean every corner of the house, and maintain it that way throughout the selling process.

FSBO homes' buyers have huge expectations, and the last thing they want is buying a house that requires a lot of improvements. Therefore, the fewer repairs found in FSBO homes, the more prospective buyers and offers you'll get.

Price Your House

One of the main reasons why FSBO homes fail to sell is overpricing the home. Homeowners find it hard to price their property because of the personal attachment.

The correct way to price the home is by getting in touch with experts such as real estate agents and appraisers. They have been in the real estate business for an extended period to have the skills to value investment properties properly.

Also, don't ignore the value of the real estate market analysis. FSBO homes' sellers want to conduct an intensive real estate market analysis to get a clue of selling prices for similar homes.

List Your Home

In a traditional real estate transaction, a real estate agent would be accountable for this task. When selling FSBO homes on your own, the property owner has to research to get several websites that permit posting homes for sale online. Overall, these kinds of sites charge a flat rate, plus the cost of essential services, such as listing yard signs and photos.

The best and most comprehensive list of real estate investment homes for sale in the US is the "Multiple Listing Service." It is accessible to realtors and some potential buyers. However, only those real estate agents with a license can list properties on MLS.

Market Your Home

After you're done listing your home, next is to market the investment property and expose it to prospective buyers as possible. Most homeowners don't have a formal network of contacts to spread the news, and putting up "For Sale" signs isn't enough. So, homeowners can market their FSBO properties by posting ads on Craigslist, creating brochures, and developing websites for their investment properties.

While marketing highlights the critical qualities of the properties to buyers. By highlighting these features, it will result in more success. You can write about everything that could make someone interested in purchasing your house. Also, post pictures of the property that capture the attractive features to potential buyers.

Show Your Home

Once you have listed and marketed the investment property, and the calls start to come in, homeowners will need to look for time to show the home to as many potential buyers as possible. It can be hard sometimes to set aside this time. However, real estate investors must remember that every viewing they skip is a lost opportunity. Therefore, ensure you can be around to fit the buyer's schedule, NOT yours.

The fact that FSBO homes should be attractive and clean has already been said before, but it is worth repeating. Make the house as beautiful as possible and set a great atmosphere that will keep people relaxed and happy while viewing the home. These good feelings can be the difference.

Also, avoid talking negatively. Don't focus on the home's problems, but again don't lie about them.

Negotiations

In real estate, negotiations are like a contract submitted to the seller. An FSBO seller can accept this offer, or analyze the contract and send it to the buyer. This process continues until both parties reach an agreement and sign the contract. In many states, homeowners would manage to get a standard contract for the transaction. If you're not familiar with the contract, you should have it checked by a real estate attorney.

In some situations, real estate agents prefer to close deals fast so they can get their commission, even if this implies not receiving the best price for the seller. For that reason, doing your own negotiations when selling FSBO houses ensures that you get the selling price you like.

Close the Transaction

Ensuring that a prospective buyer is ready to buy the investment property is a crucial element to succeed when selling FSBO homes. This is another role that real estate agents play when representing sellers in the transaction.

In the for sale by owner, the property owner must assume this responsibility and realize that not all potential buyers will be ready to purchase an investment property.

Before you close the transaction, homeowners must confirm that a prospective buyer can afford the home. The right way of doing this is by ensuring the buyer is pre-approved for a mortgage.

Lastly, when the homeowners get an offer, agree on the price and requirements with the buyer and make sure that the buyer is qualified to buy investment properties.

Selling Using Seller Financing

Seller financing, as defined in the previous chapter, is when the seller of an investment property finances the buyer to complete a real estate transaction. The real estate seller doesn't hand over cash to the buyer but instead extends credit for the real estate transaction. The buyer then makes monthly mortgage payments. Compared to a traditional home mortgage, the payments for this strategy are amortized over a given period. In most cases, a certain fraction of the investment property is amortized over the period, and then, in the end, a balloon payment for the rest of the price is paid.

Owner Financing Promissory Note

Every detail about the seller financing is captured in an agreement known as a promissory note. This is a promise that one party will pay the other party a set sum of cash when purchasing a home. A promissory note also captures what will happen in case the person buying a home defaults on payments.

Why should you consider this option when closing a real estate deal?

There are different ways in which real estate investors can gain from selling a home with owner financing:

Generate Passive Income

Owner financing is a great way to generate passive income.

Save Some Money

As long as the real estate investor is holding onto an investment property, all of the costs that come with it will have to be paid. This includes the general costs of investment property and carrying costs. If the property remains on the real estate market for too long, it can affect the overall profit on investment, depending on the investment strategy and property. So, quick selling with owner financing would be an advantage in this case. Giving buyers the option of owner financing will likely give you an upper hand.

The 1031 Exchange Strategy

This strategy references the Internal Revenue Code. While it could be new to you or your accountant, the 1031 exchange rule was established back in 1954 as an amendment of Section 112(b)(1) of the tax code. Typically, the 1031 exchange supports the tax-deferred exchange of like-kind property within specific circumstances. Virtually all property types are allowed.

Like-Kind Requirement

A real estate investor can exchange any investment property for like-kind property and avoid the capital gains tax on the sale of the first property. According to the IRS, properties belong to the like-kind if they're of the same nature, even if they vary in grade or quality. There's no limit on the number of like-kind 1031 exchanges that can be implemented in a lifetime, and there's no cap on capital gains tax that's postponed. The best thing is that an investor can defer the capital gains tax forever.

Time Restrictions

Different time restrictions are set on the investor who wants to benefit from the 1031 exchange. The first valuable time restriction is that once you sell a property, you need to find properties or property that you want to invest in within 45 days of the first property's closing date. This rule allows you to identify up to three properties.

The crucial second-time requirement of Section 1031 is that you must own the exchanged property within 180 days of the first property's closing date.

Based on these time restrictions, it is essential to remember that the day count is actual days and not business days. In other words, you have over a month and a half to identify your next property and around six months to close on the new feature.

Maintain Title in the Same Name

The claims to all the properties you buy and sell as 1031 exchange must be named with the same taxpayer's name. This should be taken literally, also. You cannot buy your first property under your personal taxpayer name and then purchase your exchange property under your new business name. Also, you cannot include your spouse to the title names, either. If you do any of these things will disqualify you from being able to claim the transaction as a 1031 exchange.

Secrets and Tricks for Selling Your Products

There are several proven ways of successfully striking a deal with a buyer. These tactics need to be practiced and polished through trial and error to get the best out of them.

It is important to stress that sales are an art, and it takes a lot of patience to make it work in your favor. There will be moments when you think it is not going your way, but you cannot give up in those struggling times. Sales involve perseverance, and if you're tenacious, you'll be a great salesperson.

Whether you're working with a wholesaler or with another organization in a significant business deal, these tips will be helpful to make the deal go more in your favor.

Make Your Agenda and Goals Clear

Most salespeople begin on the wrong foot and fail to define their intentions from the onset. When you contact your business partner, always start by making clear the agenda of the meeting. As such, both parties will know what will be covered. Keeping your customers aware of the whole process will instill trust and confidence in them to work for you.

Know Your Buyers, Products, and Services

Those working in sales mainly interact with customers, always looking for new clients to buy their products and services. Therefore, communication skill is an essential skill in this profession, but you can only communicate what you know. If you do not fully understand the product or service you are selling, then you will appear like a numbers only person who sees every client only as a source of income.

When you fail to tell what your buyer wants from you, then you're only telling them what you want to hear, not what they want to hear. Successful salespeople make large sales because they can define their products and services. They can accurately know the benefits customers will have in owning a specific product.

Understand Your Budget Early

Whenever you get into a conversation with prospective customers, try to identify relevant information as soon as you can. For instance, the price the customer is ready to pay for your products and services. In most cases, a business will speak with a prospective client, and after having a long and detailed conversation, the topic of the budget emerges.

Sometimes, you can discuss to identify a middle ground between the price at which you expect to sell and the price at which the customer will purchase. But that is not always the case. When a customer's budget is just far too low with yours, it can be very demoralizing to hear, particularly after a very long discussion.

Understand the Timeline of Your Customers

Another critical factor to consider is the customer's timeline. "When is a customer able to purchase my goods?" The sooner they can purchase, the more weight you can place on the deal. You should only invest time in an agreement the customer or business partner displays the same amount of interest as you do.

The number of deals and sales can quickly determine success in your real estate business. By closing more real estate deals in less time, it doesn't mean you cut corners. Successful real estate investors know that time is money and strive to generate qualified leads to make sure they work only with those who are worth their time and efforts.

Chapter 10: How to Get More Done by Working Less

Getting more done by working less is not only possible with real estate, but it's also quite easy to achieve once you master all the moving parts of the business. Becoming a real estate investor provides you with different profitable investment plans to choose from. However, the learning curve of real estate isn't steep as other sectors. Even investors with the least qualification can try to generate a high profit on their first investment.

Be the Boss

Achieving financial freedom that you dream of can only be realized through a meticulous and organized plan. Here are a few steps and tips that will guide you on how to become the boss.

1. Set Specific Objectives

The most common real estate investing mistake that novice investors make is to avoid to set objectives before starting a business venture. The significance of fixed goals cannot be understated. In fact, having a well-thought idea of what you want to achieve is one of the marks of a detailed plan.

2. Choose a Real Estate Investment Strategy

The next step is to select an approach that suits your needs. Real estate presents numerous strategies that differ in terms of their level of risks, complexity, and time horizon.

3. Spend Time to Master Your Strategy

Once you pick an investment strategy, you must commit time to master everything about it. With the resources available nowadays, acquiring extensive knowledge about the market has become a simple process.

4. Use Leverage

Leverage helps you to pay a fraction of the total cost of the investment property. This effectively reduces the barrier to entry for investors with little budgets and allows them to take advantage of the available capital.

5. Narrow Your Investment

Once you identify a working formula, the next logical step is to repeat the process on a broader scale. As your income grows, continue to add different types of investment properties to your portfolio to make sure there is steady and continuous growth.

All things factored, real estate investing stands out as the best and effective way to attain financial independence.

Being Effective vs. Being Efficient

Many words exist in the English language that has very similar meanings but used differently.

The two words effective vs. efficient are among those words. They both mean "having an effect," but each word has its unique application.

The word effective is concerned with whether or not something is achieved. It doesn't concentrate on how something is done, but instead, if it is done at all.

On the other hand, the word efficient is concerned with how something is done. Was it accomplished with little waste or expense?

When it comes to matters to do with productivity, many people and organizations work hard to be more efficient. They want to finish most of the to-do list items per day, reach out to more leads per month, or do something in less time.

If you're wondering about whether to become effective or efficient, it is vital first to understand what efficiency and effectiveness mean as well as the outcome of being efficient versus being effective.

Based on the early definition, you're more efficient if you discover a way to do something two times or five times in the time it used to take you to do it once.

For example, an efficient way to reach out to a lot of deals is to broadcast mass emails, all with the same marketing text. This way, you can reach out to thousands of leads per day.

Now, let's turn out attention to what effectiveness is. If your original goal is to generate a sale, a mass email blast is usually effective. For sure, you reach out too many people at once, but how many times do they open and read your marketing email, even click through, and buy what you're selling?

A more effective approach to accomplish a real sale is to take the time to research a prospective client or customer and send them a personalized email explaining how your product may help their specific situation with a few tips on how they could implement it. They're likely to respond to such a message with obvious steps than to a generic message. The great thing is that you will have achieved one sale, even if it consumed your afternoon, or even longer to craft it.

These, however, are the two best examples to help you understand the difference between being effective and being efficient. While you should strive to be effective first, you also need to consider whether you're making use of your time and resources.

The Number 1 Enemy of Progress

Many people do not realize this, but one of the most precious commodities for human beings is *Time*. Yes! You can always make more money, but you can't always create more *Time*...can you?

Two of the biggest challenges we face in real estate investing are *Time* and *Complacency*.

Complacency costs real estate investors hundreds of thousands of dollars or even millions during their investing career because they become "Comfortable."

It's said, "comfort is the enemy of progress," and it's never been truer than in Real Estate Investing. The rental checks are flowing every month, why rock the boat. Wrong!!

Therefore, to make it in real estate investing, don't lose your edge. Stay engaged and don't let comfort to cost you millions.

Conclusion

While there are many questions you should be asking yourself, it is my best opinion that the level of your success as a real estate investor will be directly proportional to the time and answers you arrive at in responding to the questions.

Taking the time to "do it right" at the start will eliminate many, many problems down the road and simplify your transition into the world of successful real estate investors.

Success on your real estate investment journey starts with learning. The goal of this book is to provide you with a great foundation to get started in your real estate investing career.

House Flipping
- Beginners Guide

The Ultimate Fix and Flip Strategies on How to Find, Buy, Fix, and Then Sell at a Profit to Achieve Financial Freedom from Real Estate Investing

David Hewitt & Andrew Peter

Introduction

House flipping programs on HGTV and other cable networks have inspired a keen interest in real estate investment. The good news is that real estate investing still remains one of the best ways to create wealth and build residual income over time. However, there is still a science to it. It's not like you can jump in and buy a house, paint a few walls, and then expect to flip that home for profit. There is research involved. You need to know the market, how to negotiate, how to build a budget, and close on a sale, just to name a few things. This book is designed to guide you through the process of house flipping, from preparing your financing options to the close.

The high demand of the market creates the perfect opportunity for a new real estate investor to purchase and sell houses quickly, increasing the profit margin. In some hot markets across the country, homes can sell in 3-7 days. Chief economist for the National Association of Realtors, Lawrence Yun, predicted that new home sales will increase by 21% in 2021, increasing wealth of homeowners (Orton, 2021). This presents an incredible opportunity for existing and potential estate investors, which is one of the reasons I wrote this book.

This book is designed to walk you through all of the necessary steps to launch a successful career as a house flipper and real estate investor. Given the unpredictability of our market, building assets through real estate can provide you with the financial stability you need to weather the storm. We will walk you through the basic concepts of house flipping in case this is a concept that is completely new to you. From there, we will show you all of the steps necessary to procure your first property, from securing your financing to working with realtors and other industry experts. What you will learn early in this process is there is a lot of research involved. We understand that it's not a very sexy part of the job, but without it, you won't have a flip, so please take the steps in the process seriously. After you've done your research, you can start searching for the right property. We will educate you on the different types of properties and where you should buy as a new investor. After you've found your first property, you're going to run some numbers to see if this property is the best option for you. That's where we'll introduce the flip formula to guide your math. After you've chosen your property and made your offer—which we'll walk you through as well—you can build your scope of work, which will be the first steps to outlining your budget and schedule. We cover all of this and more in this guidebook.

If you are willing to put in the necessary sweat equity and follow the steps in this book, you will be on your way to creating wealth as a house flipper. Now is the perfect time to grab your real estate market share. Time is of the essence, as you never know how long markets stay hot for or when they cool down. If you want to ride the rising real estate wave that is cresting, the time is now to learn.

In this book, we will outline these twenty steps to launch you into your first rehab:

1. Defining the concept of house flipping.

2. Preparing your financing.

3. Finding an agent to work with.

4. Determining where you should buy.

5. What kind of property should you buy?

6. Who to buy from.

7. How to find deals.

8. Your flip formula.

9. Looking at properties.

10. Making offers.

11. Your due diligence.

12. Creating your SOW.

13. Creating your budget.

14. Creating your schedule.

15. Hiring contractors.

16. Managing your rehab.

17. Using an agent or For Sale By Owner.

18. Staging.

19. Buyer due diligence.

20. The closing.

Chapter One: First Concepts

Before you jump into your first house flip, it's important that you understand some of the basic fundamentals of house flipping, starting with the basic definition. Flipping a house simply means that you purchase it with the intent of selling it quickly to earn a profit (How to flip a house, 2020). When the real estate climate is fertile for house flipping, house sales rise. If the market has created an environment where more people want to own an asset, the people will likely take advantage of the lower interest rates to invest in a home. Also during some specific events, people may want to spend more time at home, also creating more of a demand for home sales. It's good to infer people's attitude toward current global and local events. The result? Real estate investing and house flipping is more relevant today than it has ever been.

Can you make a good living as a house flipper? That depends upon your market and how many houses you can flip each year. If you can manage a consistent rehab schedule, which we will discuss later in this book, you can earn a strong income as a house flipper. The general rule of thumb is that you don't want to invest in a property that won't yield you 10-15% in profit after expenses. Anything less than this is costing you money rather than making it. Although the range is variable, experienced flippers usually hope to earn at least $25,000 per flip (Home Shows, How much do house flippers make). As a novice flipper, you can expect to earn a little less than this, but just follow the formula of the 10-15% I mentioned earlier, and you should be just fine.

As a new house flipper, you will be earning your income in lump sums. Therefore, it is important that you are privy to tax rules, as they imply to real estate investing to avoid a potential audit. The IRS does not consider real estate investing to be passive income, but active income. The result? You'll be placed in a higher tax bracket, resulting in 10% - 37%. You'll also be subject to self-employment tax. As you are planning your income, it is imperative that you factor these expenses in (Ivy, 2019).

Many new house flippers wonder how viable it is to flip houses part-time. Although you want the financial benefits of house flipping, you don't want to give up a potential steady income if you have a full-time job. Can you flip houses part-time? The short answer to this question is yes. It is a simple way to get started in this business at a low risk. It is important to understand that if you are flipping part-time, your rehabs will typically take longer because you are splitting your time. That means you will not be able to flip as many homes as you would if you were a full-time investor, also meaning that your income potential will be less (Kidd, Is flipping houses part-time or on the side possible). If you are just looking to make a part-time, side hustle income, then this is fine. However, if you would like to build a full-time income from house flipping, you will need to plan a transition to work as an investor full-time to capitalize on your full income potential.

Chapter Summary

- Definition of house flipping.

- Relevancy of house flipping in your market.

- Money you can earn as a house flipper.

- Taxes and house flipping.

- House flipping part-time.

In the next chapter, you will learn how to prepare your financing for your first flip.

Chapter Two: Preparing Your Financing

Now that you understand the basics of house flipping, it's important that you review your finance options when buying your first house.

Hard money loan. You can approach a bank for a traditional loan for your first house. Depending upon interest rates, this may be a viable option for house flippers with a strong credit score.

Friends and family. If you don't want to resort to a loan or lack the collateral or credit score to secure funding, consider approaching your friends and family for fiscal support. If you present this to them as an investment where they will receive a return, you might be surprised at the level of support you will receive. Pitch it as a way for them to earn money, too.

Cash out on existing investments like home equity or 401k. If you have equity in your own home, you could consider a home equity loan to fund your first flip. If you've been at your job for a while, you could also borrow against your 401k to fund your first project.

Partner with another investor. If you know other investors or network with other real estate investors, consider a partnership. If you don't mind splitting the profit, you could work with another investor that could provide funding while you put in the sweat equity. You could even consider taking a lesser percentage to work with a more experienced house flipper, so you can learn more on the job and earn your first lump sum.

Chapter Summary

- Options to secure financing for your first flip.

- Secure a hard money loan.

- Ask friends and family.

- Cash out on investments.

- Partner with another investor.

In the next chapter, you will learn how to secure a real estate agent or become one yourself.

Chapter Three: Find Your Agent(s)

To access the best real estate deals, especially in a market where supply is limited, it is important to find and partner with real estate agents in your market. When searching for a real estate agent to work with, you will want one who is investor-friendly.

An investor-friendly agent is defined as "a licensed real estate professional who has experience with real estate properties, has worked with investors, and has knowledge of the local market. Said agent will be an investor, as well. They will help find deals, analyze them, make offers, and sell properties as necessary" (Shields, Do you need an investor friendly agent to buy an investment property).

If you would like to pocket all of your profit on your real estate deals, you might want to consider becoming a real estate agent yourself. Although getting your license will require some investment in time and education, it can benefit your business in several ways.

- It will provide more visibility to investment opportunities. As an agent, you will have access to the MLS, which will allow you to see homes on the market, sometimes before they are available to the public.

- Becoming an agent opens up another revenue opportunity for you as an investor. You will earn a 6% commission on each house you sell, increasing your investment profit margin. If you're not an agent, you will have to give up this income and factor that into your overall profit on each deal. There may also be other deals available that you may not invest in but sell, enabling you to earn a 6% commission.

- Being your agent gives you more leverage on the entire deal because you are in control of the entire process.

- Agents are required to invest in continuing education to keep your license active. This is beneficial to you as an investor because you will stay up to date on the market and changes as they happen (Real Estate Express, 5 Advantages of Getting a License for Real Estate Investment)

Chapter Summary

- Consider an investor-friendly real estate agent.

- Get your real estate license to create a secondary income and leverage your investment deals.

In the next chapter, you will learn how to farm an area and determine where to buy.

Chapter Four: Where You Should Buy

In real estate, the name of the game is location, location, location. Once you partner with an agent or become one yourself, it is imperative that you find the best locations to buy. It will do you no good to buy a house at $50,000 if all the homes in the neighborhood sell for no more than $60,000. You want to make a profit. There is a science to this process. You want to find neighborhoods and areas that are on the rise, where you can find a home at a great rate, flip it, and sell it for an amazing profit. So how do you find these golden opportunities? How do you know where to buy?

This is where you will have to tap into your left brain analytics. Start the process by reviewing market information for your area. If you are partnered with a real estate agent, they can assist you with this, but you will also want to supplement their work. Of course, if you've chosen to get licensed yourself, you can use resources like the MLS to fuel your research. But the options are vast. Learn about the market around you from the local newspaper, the Census Bureau, and the National Association of Realtors. Learn about the demographics of each market, such as the median income and how homes are selling. Review historical data on the neighborhood and home you are considering. This will provide insight into whether your market is trending up or down. You don't want to buy a home that has been losing value over the years.

Next, you want to research the market status. Is it a rental or a buyer's market? How long are homes staying on the market before they rent or sell? This will provide considerable insight into how your investment will fare, should you choose to flip there. The state of the market will often dictate whether you're in a buyers or sellers market. For example, after the 2008 market crash, the sellers' market decreased, but the renters market was on fire. Since so many people were losing their jobs and foreclosure rates were high, people were afraid to invest in homes. Lenders were not handing out loans, and the market just was not buyer-friendly. You need to watch for current trends in the world and market. During certain trends and happenings in the world, interest rates may fluctuate. That is why it's important to do your research.

Calculate your cash on cash return. "It lets you compare annual cash income against the cash you invested..to calculate your cash on cash return, divide your annual pre-tax cash flow by cash invested" (Moore, The Beginner's Guide to Real Estate Market Analysis).

As you are calculating your cash on return, consider your expenses. If you've done accurate research on your neighborhood, you should be well-informed on what kind of finishes and upgrades to include in your flip. For example, you don't want to invest in granite or quartz in a lower income neighborhood where laminate would do just fine. The goal is to earn a return on your income plus profit. That means you sometimes have to take your personal taste and preference out of it. Be practical and make choices that are going to put money into your pocket and not take it away.

Chapter Summary

- Conduct a market analysis of your area to learn demographics and historical data.

- Are you in a renters or buyers market? Know your market conditions.

- Calculate cash on cash return.

- Evaluate expenses of your flip and match your upgrades with your neighborhood.

In the next chapter, you will learn what kind of properties you should buy.

Chapter Five: What You Should Buy

Once you have learned about the market, it is now time to determine what kind of property you should buy. There are several options to consider. You could buy distressed properties, foreclosed properties, or retail properties. There are pros and cons to each. Let's take a moment to look into each of these options to determine which would be best for you.

Distressed properties. "A distressed property is a property that is on the brink of foreclosure or already owned by the bank" (Johnson, 2020). Though distressed properties provide a way to make higher profit since you can buy them at a discount, it is a tightrope when trying to balance the cost versus the expenses. It is possible that you may find distressed property in a great neighborhood where homes are selling like hotcakes, but the house needs so much work that you don't stand to make a profit. In cases like this, you don't want to become jaded by smoke and mirrors and walk out losing money. For the most part, distressed properties are a great option to consider when flipping a house, but you want to consider some criteria when evaluating this option.

- Know the market value of your neighborhood. One of the best benefits of distressed properties is low cost, but how low? Make sure you stand to make a profit when buying a distressed property. If the highest valued home in the neighborhood is $80,000, then a $70,000 property is not a good buy.

- Be prepared for a large investment. Distressed properties require more TLC. You need to make sure you have the proper investment budget to make the home sellable.

- Be prepared for unexpected risks. Like any flip, you want to have a contingency. Many problems hide beneath the surface of the home like termites, septic issues, and asbestos. Unfortunately, these problems are also the most costly. Be prepared (Clothier, 4 must- knows before taking on a distressed property).

Foreclosed properties. There are some similarities between distressed properties and foreclosed properties, since both are owned by the bank. The good news with foreclosed properties is all foreclosed properties are not necessarily in bad shape, and you can purchase them below market value. You can also secure good financing options on these homes because the banks are eager to unload them. However, like distressed properties, you want to go into these deals with your eyes open and a strategy to ensure you walk away with a profit. When buying foreclosed homes, be prepared for the following:

- High competition. Who doesn't want to buy a house at a discounted rate? The high competition among investors can often lead to a bidding war, which means you may have to spend more money out of pocket than anticipated. The heightened competition can also extend your buying process, which will extend your overall timeline on the project.

- Not always ideal for the novice investor. Although foreclosed properties seem like a great way to get started, it's not an ideal start for a new investor. Dealing with the banks and coming up with the best offers takes time and experience. Foreclosed properties also carry more risk, which a new investor won't be able to afford (Hamed, 2018).

Retail properties. The last option to consider are your retail properties. These opportunities are a bit more cut and dry compared to your distressed and foreclosed properties. There is less risk involved, as these homes usually require less work, but they will often require a higher upfront investment. That simply means you need to brush up on your negotiating skills as a new investor. This is also where partnering up with a real estate agent or becoming one yourself will come in handy. Access to homes through tools like the MLS will reveal deals you would be unable to find otherwise.

Chapter Summary

- Evaluate different options for buying: retail, distressed, foreclosed homes.

- Distressed homes can be bought at a discount but may carry more risk.

- Foreclosed homes are great buys but come with a lot of competition and may not be ideal for novice investors.

- Retail properties provide less risk for a new investor and can partner well with a real estate agent.

In the next chapter, you will learn who to buy your investment property from.

Chapter Six: Who to Buy From

When evaluating who to buy your investment property from, there are two basic categories: bank-owned or private seller. The most important characteristic to consider when evaluating your seller is that you want someone who is motivated.

Private sellers. The majority of homes that you will purchase will be from private sellers. If you are evaluating homes with an agent and using tools like the MLS, you will be able to identify various deals that can fit your specific needs. You may be wondering what exactly qualifies someone as a motivated seller.

- Home has been on the market for an extended period of time. If your seller's home has been sitting on the market for a long time, they are going to be motivated to get rid of it. This will give you leverage to negotiate a lower rate. However, before you jump into a deal, make sure you investigate why the home has been on the market for so long. The answers you find may be the difference between you making a deal or walking away.

- Estate sale. When a family member has passed away and the family is sorting out the details of their estate, they are often motivated to sell so they can move on with their lives.

- Seller has already purchased another home. No one wants to carry a double mortgage. Once your seller has bought another home, they are on a race to sell their old home as quickly as possible to avoid paying two mortgages.

Bank-owned properties. If you opt to purchase distressed or foreclosed properties, you will have to work with a bank. As mentioned previously, this will require a higher level of skill in negotiating, which is not ideal for a new investor. It is recommended that if you purchase a bank-owned property that you work with someone with more experience, such as another investor or real estate agent.

Chapter Summary

- Buy your first home from a private owner or the bank.

- You want to buy from a motivated seller

- Consider partnering up with an experienced investor or agent on bank-owned properties.

In the next chapter, you will learn how to find deals.

Chapter Seven: How You'll Find Deals

Now that you know the types of properties that exist in the marketplace, it is time to find your own deals. Being a successful investor hinges upon utilizing the resources available to you. One of the first things you want to do is identify your niche so you can develop a strategy. Know what type of property you are going after, whether it is retail, foreclosed, or distressed. Know the area you want to focus and how you want to plan to approach it.

Once you've identified your foundation, you will want to start your search. There are a number of ways to find your deals. Try several and stick with the ones that work the best for you.

Networking. Between online marketplaces and local area groups, you can uncover good deals by networking with other professionals in the industry. It will also help you find allies that will work with you long-term on finding deals, so this experience is invaluable. If you're an introvert, we're sorry, but it's time to get out of your comfort zone.

Maximize the MLS. You should have access to the MLS, whether it is through a real estate agent you're partnered with or you've chosen to become a license agent yourself. Some flags to look for when reviewing these listings include: homes that have been on the listing for an extended period of time, homes that were removed and relisted, and expired listings. These are going to be opportunities where the seller is motivated and ready to strike a deal with you.

Partner with wholesalers. Wholesalers are motivated to help you find the motivated sellers you need. You will have to share your profit or provide a finding fee when working with them, but they will bring you opportunities you would otherwise not find.

Mortgage brokers and title companies. These guys are in the know about who is actively selling and buying. Building an alliance with them will allow you to uncover more off-market deals.

Grassroots driving for dollars. There's no better way to uncover opportunities than just driving around your neighborhoods to see what is for sale. There is more to this process than just driving by. Put your interviewing skills to the test and talk to neighbors in the area. Learn more about the neighborhood and opportunities that might come available.

Advertising. Post signs around your neighborhood. Invest in a direct mail campaign and consider online ads to drive leads for deals (Rohde, 2021).

Chapter Summary

- Identify your niche and build a strategy.

- Network to find off-market deals.

- Utilize the MLS.

- Drive for a dollar.

- Invest in advertising.

In the next chapter, you will learn the flip formula.

Chapter Eight: The Flip Formula

In real estate investing, a little math is involved. Don't worry, it's not that complicated, but you do want to know how much money you need to invest in each flip and how much profit you stand to make. These calculations need to be done on the front end to determine if the deal is right for you.

The first thing you need to know as a house flipper is the 70% rule. "The 70% rule says that an investor should spend no more than 70% of a property's after repair value (ARV) on a property. This includes the price you pay for the property itself, as well as any estimated repair costs" (Ball, 2020).

You want to start with determining your ARV. You can determine this by shopping the comps in the area. Multiply your ARV by 0.7 to determine your 70% figure. Next, you want to deduct your anticipated repair costs, which you would receive from your contractor from your 70% number.

For example, let's assume your ARV is $250,000.

Multiply 250,000 by .70, which equals $175,000.

You would talk to your contractor, and they will tell you that your repair costs will be $50,000. Subtract this number from your 70% number, which leaves you with $125,000. This is your maximum purchase price to turn a profit on this deal (How to flip houses...as simple as 5th grade math).

Chapter Summary

- Follow the 70% rule to make a profit

- Determine your ARV and follow the 70% formula to learn your max spending on a property.

In the next chapter, you will learn how to look at properties.

Chapter Nine: Looking at Properties

As you search for the perfect house to flip, there will be characteristics that you will want to consider beyond just the location. Physical characteristics play an important role in determining if your potential flip is viable.

The first thing you want to do is compare your potential flip with comparable homes in the area. Is it a 2-bedroom home when all the other houses in the neighborhood have three bedrooms? This is important to know because it will affect the overall market value of the home.

As you are observing physical characteristics of the house, look for areas that need work. This is an indication that it might be a good flip property. Does the lawn look overgrown and neglected? Does it look like it's been a while since someone has lived there?

Take the time to tour other homes in the area to see the pros and cons of your competition. Be creative when coming up with ways to leverage your flip, but make reasonable choices that don't step outside of the scope of the neighborhood; otherwise, you risk compromising your profit potential (How to choose a house to flip).

Chapter Summary

- Research your competition.

- Observe physical characteristics of the home.

- Be creative in your rehab solutions.

In the next chapter, you will learn how to make your first offer.

Chapter Ten: Making Offers

As you get ready to make your first offer on your flip, preparation is key. Know exactly what you want and what you are trying to accomplish. Establish your goals for the deal and be prepared to stick by those goals.

- It's okay to walk away. Although it may be easy to get attached to your first property, it is more important that you're attached to your budget. Be prepared to walk away if you are unable to negotiate the right numbers for your deal.

- Give the last concession in the negotiating process to maintain your posture. Whether it is closing costs or something else, you will likely go back and forth with the seller. Make sure you say the last word and offer the last concession.

- Distract your seller with a red herring tactic. Take the focus off the actual negotiating price and tilt it toward something else, like an item in the home that you'd like to convey.

- Penalize the seller for asking for multiple concessions. This is more of a training technique than anything else to let the seller know that you won't budge on your offer.

- Stand by your numbers. If you are working with an experienced negotiator, they will do their best to sway you from your set numbers. You walked in with a goal in mind. You know what you're trying to accomplish and exactly what you'll need to accomplish that goal. Don't falter.

- Don't get offended. You never know how a seller might react to your offer. Don't take anything personally. Keep it professional. If they want to remain in the deal, they will stay at the table. Keep your poker face on.

- Use data. Half of your job as an investor is analytics. Use those to your advantage at the negotiating table. Justify your actions through numbers (Turner, 13 tips for real estate negotiation).

Chapter Summary

- Be prepared at the negotiating table.

- Know what you want and stick to your numbers.

In the next chapter, you will learn about due diligence.

Chapter Eleven: Your Due Diligence

Before we dive into this chapter, let's first define due diligence. Due diligence is "investigation or audit of a potential or product to confirm all of the facts" (Syrios, The ultimate guide to due diligence). Research is imperative to successful real estate investment. Without proper due diligence, you risk sabotaging your deal. Don't skip this step. There's nothing fun or sexy about due diligence, but it's necessary.

Here are the areas you must consider in your due diligence efforts:

- **Area analysis.** You want to make sure the area you chose will yield you a profit. Research your area thoroughly. Do the math. Conduct your AMV to see what properties make sense and which ones don't. Know how much your rehab will cost. Lack of due diligence in this area would be extremely costly.

- **Physical inspections.** When looking at a home, make sure your due diligence is expansive. You might be looking at homes that need a lot of work, but make sure the amount of work needed doesn't exceed the anticipated budget.

- **Know your money.** Make sure your budget is reasonable based on the research you've already done. Run all the numbers to make sure everything makes sense and you stand to make a profit before going to the negotiating table.

- Never skip an inspection. Inspections will reveal things about the house that you can't see on the surface. You don't want to get stuck with a home that has structural issues and will cost you thousands of dollars because you neglected your due diligence on the inspection side (Syrios, The ultimate guide to due diligence).

Chapter Summary

- Don't skip due diligence, even though it may seem boring.

- Due diligence pre-offer.

- Due diligence post-offer.

In the next chapter, you will learn how to create your scope of work.

Chapter Twelve: Create Your SOW

Your SOW, or rehab scope of work, is the blueprint to properly managing your rehab. Building a scope of work is essential to maximizing your profit potential, accuracy, and efficiency while minimizing your risk.

When an investor builds their SOW, it should consist of six major parts.

1. **Build an overview and description.** This is your overall summary of the entire project. It will outline general information about the property and basic components of the rehab. At the end of your overview, you will outline the contractors needed to fulfill the tasks of this rehab project.

2. **Exterior.** This is going to cover all the work that needs to be completed on the outside of the home, such as the roof, windows, landscaping, and doors, just to name a few. Anything outside the home that needs to be updated should be included in this part of the report. If the rehab includes a new fence or deck, that should be included in this section.

3. **Interior.** This will include the inside perimeter of the home, such as walls, floors, molding, and light fixtures. If walls need to be knocked down to open up an area, this will be included in this section. If walls need to be painted, carpet installed, or hardwood floors refinished, this will be included here.

4. **Kitchen.** The kitchen is often one of the most expensive rooms in a home to renovate, which is why it gets its own section. New cabinets, countertops, appliances, and backsplashes will be included here.

5. **Bathrooms.** Bathrooms are big selling features in a home and will likely be included in your scope. This section of your report will include everything from the tub/shower, toilet, vanity, light fixtures, and paint.

6. **Plumbing and electrical.** This will include everything from the outlets, hot water heater, and light switches. If you opt to add a room to the house, like a bathroom, or you plan to move a laundry room, you will have to invest in the plumbing and electrical (Merrill, How to write a rehab scope of work).

As you are building your SOW, it is important to anticipate what your buyers will like. This is why your due diligence is so important. It will reveal what is trending in the market and what is attracting buyers and driving more sales. For example, many buyers love open concept. Consider this as you are building your SOW to make sure your home is accommodating this demand. You also want to utilize as much space as possible in the home. Buyers don't like to walk into a home and see wasted space. To them, this is wasted money. Make use of all the space you have. Be creative and show your buyers how to best utilize it. Keep everything neutral. Don't allow your personal taste to interfere with your profit potential. Vanilla is best if you want to attract the most potential buyers (Merrill, How to write a rehab scope of work).

Chapter Summary

- The SOW is the blueprint for managing your rehab.

- Build your SOW based on what your buyers might like.

In thenext chapter, you will learn how to create your rehab budget.

Chapter Thirteen: Create Your Budget

We have discussed the foundations for building your rehab budget. Your due diligence includes researching comps in the area and determining how your flip matches up against them. This will enable you to calculate your ARV and assist you in determining what a reasonable budget for your flip should be.

Once you've determined your ARV, conduct a walkthrough of your property with a contractor to assess the repairs that need to be made to reach your ARV and earn your maximum profit. The contractor will be able to assess what your total budget will be for the rehab. Don't forget to include a contingency in your budget to account for surprises. As soon as you begin the rehab process and start to open up walls, you're likely to run into repair issues that you did not account for. This is why a contingency is necessary. 10% is a reasonable amount of contingency to include in your budget. It's like an insurance policy—you may not use all of it, but you do want to be prepared (Correctly estimating your rehab budget).

Chapter Summary

- Conduct your due diligence and calculate your ARV.

- Walk through your property with a contractor to itemize your expenses.

In the next chapter, you will learn how to create your schedule.

Chapter Fourteen: Create Your Schedule

Creating the schedule for your flip is essential to maximizing your income potential. The longer you hold the home, the more carrying costs you will incur. If you are financing your home, carrying costs include your mortgage and interest. Every month you have to pay this, it eats into your profit. Therefore, your goal is to turn the home as quickly as possible once you make a deal.

/fo+Typical flips average a six to eight week timeline, but it really varies depending upon the house and what needs to be done. Here are some basic guidelines to assist you in building your first flip schedule:

- **Inspection, 2 weeks:** Remember that you always want to have an inspection after you purchase a home. Leaving this out could end up costing you more money, so please make sure you do it. You want a couple of weeks to evaluate the work that needs to be done and get estimates once your inspection report is complete.

- **Project planning, 2-8 weeks:** After you have completed your inspection, this will include mapping out your entire project from start to finish, building your SOW, and hiring contractors.

- **Exterior, 1-4 weeks:** If the exterior work needed on your home is minimal, you'll likely end up on the lower end of this timeline. However, if you have extensive work, like roof repair or extensive landscaping, budget this in closer to a month.

- **Interior, 4-16 weeks:** The interior is the meat of your project, and where you'll spend the most of your time, whether you're just painting walls and refinishing floors or remodeling an entire kitchen (Learn how to create a rehab schedule).

Run through these components as you build your flip schedule to determine how much time it will take to complete your rehab.

Chapter Summary

- Maximize your profit with an effective rehab schedule.

- Estimate the time to complete each component of the rehab, from inspection to interior work.

In the next chapter, you will learn how to hire contractors.

Chapter Fifteen: Hiring Contractors

The contractors you choose for your flip can make or break your project. Choosing the wrong contractor can result in loss of profit, and in some cases, even forfeit the entire flip. We are not telling you this as a scare tactic; it is important that you take the process of hiring your contractors seriously. You need to take your time to ensure this process is done right because there are a lot of bad contractors out there that will steal your money, but the good thing is that there are a lot of good contractors too. Consider these suggestions as you interview your contractors, and you will be well on your way to a successful flip with a strong team you can use over and over again.

- **Always get references.** But, don't just stop at references from the contractor themselves. Of course they are going to refer you to people that make them look good. You need outside references beyond who they refer you to. Ideally, a reference from someone you know or trust works best, but before you hire the contractor, just make sure you get references from more sources than who they give you. As a rule of thumb, three to five references are acceptable.

- **Interview at least three contractors.** You want to interview and get quotes from at least three contractors. It doesn't matter if you feel a special connection with the first one you meet. Stick to the rule of three. You cannot make an informed decision with just one bid.

- **Compare each contractor.** Write down what you like about each contractor and what you don't like. Make sure they are apples to apples comparisons. One contractor might be more expensive but bring more to the table than the other two. How valuable is that to you? Keep a detailed list to help you make an informed decision once the process is over.

- **Make sure your contractors are licensed and insured.** This is self explanatory and will serve to protect you and your project. This should be non-negotiable.

- **Treat the process like a job interview.** If you don't like the way the contractor communicates, and they show up late for your first appointment, you probably don't want to work with them. Professionalism is necessary.

- **Know their payment terms.** Get their payment terms in writing at the outset of your relationship. Make sure it is clear what is expected on both sides. Do you pay half up front and half after the job is done? Whatever you agree to, make sure it is reasonable and to the benefit of you both (Naftulin, 2016).

Following these steps as you prepare to hire your contractors will not only serve you well on this flip, but for future flips too. It may require that you invest a bit of time upfront, but isn't it worth it if you can build your team of contractors now and not have to do it again? It's possible if you take the time to hire correctly.

Chapter Summary

- Your contractors will make or break your flip.

- Take your time hiring the right contractors, and you might never have to do it again.

- Interview your contractors like they're on a job interview.

In the next chapter, you will learn how to manage your rehab.

Chapter Sixteen: Managing Your Rehab

If you follow all the steps outlined in this book, you should have no problem managing your rehab. Having a strong scope of work and a schedule to follow will ensure that you have a blueprint to follow throughout the process. Stick to this blueprint. That doesn't mean you cannot allow room for flexibility, but the further you veer away from your timeline, the more it will eat into your overall profit. The best way to make sure you stay on track with your schedule is to have strong contractors. We reviewed in the last chapter the importance of hiring great contractors and the impact they can have on your project. Good contractors are good for their word, and you can trust them to complete their tasks when they say they will. Bad contractors can stretch a project for days and even weeks. If you see signs of this creeping in with one of your contractors, don't hesitate to fire them. Firing a contractor does mean that you will have to invest time in finding a replacement, but how much more time and money will be lost if you continue to work with them on projects with never-ending deadlines? Don't be afraid to let a contractor go if things are not going the way they should. You will lose time in the project as a result of their performance, but not as much time as you will lose if you choose to keep them on the project.

Hiring a general contractor can help you stay on top of the project as the general contractor will be responsible for being on site everyday and overseeing every aspect of the project. Many general contractors come with their own crews because they've had experience on projects and know who works best at each task. However, like any other contractor, make sure you interview and vet them as well. You want to make sure you can trust someone you're giving that much authority to. Also, whether you have a general contractor on board or not, don't make the mistake of thinking you don't need to show up at the work site daily too. This is your project and your investment. Make sure you're present and aware of everything that is happening on your work site. You have a vested interest in everything that is going on there. One of the biggest mistakes novice flippers make is not showing up at the work site.

Chapter Summary

- Stick to your scope of work, your blueprint.

- Don't be afraid to fire a contractor if they are not performing.

- Consider hiring a general contractor.

- Show up at the worksite.

In the next chapter, you will learn whether to use an agent or for sale by owner.

Chapter Seventeen: Agent or FSBO?

We talked about the value of partnering with an agent earlier in this book, but what about for sale by owner, or FSBO? As an investor, do you have to choose? Not necessarily. There is value in utilizing both to secure good real estate deals.

First, when you are partnering with an agent, like all of your partnerships, you want to make sure they are carefully vetted. A real estate agent can be your greatest ally if chosen correctly. When searching for an agent, you are looking for someone who can do much more than just show homes. An agent needs to be:

- **A strong negotiator.** You want to work with an agent that can help you secure deals and get them at a great price. As an investor, you are looking for deals under market value, and to achieve this, you must be a master negotiator.

- **Highly responsive.** Your agent needs to be available and able to respond at a moment's notice.

- **They know the local market.** You want to work with an agent that knows the market well. They are well-researched and up to speed on everything about your local neighborhoods.

- **They know investing.** You want to work with a real estate agent who has experience working with investors. They know and understand your world and leverage themselves as an asset.

- **Network.** You want to work with an agent who is well-networked. They know other mortgage brokers and people in the industry who all have their fingers on the pulse of what is happening in the real estate market (Yale, 2019).

For sale by owner (FSBO) is more of a grassroots approach to real estate investing. You will likely run into more FSBO opportunities when you drive for dollars. One of the biggest benefits of FSBO is that you are often dealing directly with the owner and don't have to pay out a commission to an agent on the sale. The con is that you will have to do everything that a realtor would normally do, like negotiating. As a new investor, this may be a skill you have yet to develop, so it might be to your advantage to work with a realtor rather than focus on FSBO opportunities. As you build more experience as an investor and have a few deals behind you, FSBO might be a great strategy to consider.

Chapter Summary

- Agents are great allies, but take the time to properly vet them before working with them.

- Agents should be master negotiators and have experience working with investors.

- FSBO is a great grassroots opportunity, but not ideal for new investors.

In the next chapter, you will learn the importance of staging.

Chapter Eighteen: Staging

This is a step in the process that is easy for new investors to skip, simply because they don't want to spend the money. Put yourself in the buyer's shoes. How much more likely are you to buy a home that is staged versus one that is not? Have you ever visited a model home in a new construction community? The model homes always have a rich, homely feel because they want the buyers to experience what the home would feel like if it was theirs. Now let's take a look at some numbers in case you're still not convinced.

- 58% of seller's realtors said their homes sold for more money because their homes were staged.

- In a survey of 3,500 staged homes, 46% sold for 10% more.

- Homes staged pre-listed averaged less than 30 days on the market (Cohen, 2019).

The bottom line is that staging puts money back in your pocket as an investor. You could choose to DIY staging or hire a professional. As a new investor, hiring a professional is recommended because you are new to this process, and you want it done right. It is an expense to hire a professional stager, but you see the statistics on staging; it's an investment that is worth it.

Chapter Summary

- Staging is an investment that puts money back into your pocket.

- Consider hiring a professional stager for the best results.

In the next chapter, you will learn about buyer due diligence.

Chapter Nineteen: Buyer Due Diligence

Just as you conducted your due diligence when you purchased your property, you can expect your buyer to do the same. Some will be more diligent than others. Regardless, you need to be prepared to address their due diligence. If you've done your due diligence, you should have no problem matching theirs. Make sure you know what your property is worth and be prepared to stand firm on your offer. If you've prepared as you should, you will allow a degree of flexibility at the negotiating table, but it is essential that you keep your poker face and know your limit.

If your buyer has done their due diligence, they will ask for an inspection. This should not be a cause for concern if you have done your due diligence and ordered an inspection when you purchased the property and addressed any issues that came up. If, however, you left any of those issues outstanding, you must be prepared to offer concessions to your buyer once their inspection report comes back. That is the right and ethical thing to do.

The same is true of the appraisal. Proper due diligence on your part will ensure that you don't run into any problems here. If you don't get your house appraised prior to the sale, you risk losing profit if it doesn't appraise at your asking price. The bank will not finance above the appraisal, so make sure you have prepared in advance for this. Make sure your home will meet these requirements so it doesn't tie up your deal.

It is also possible that your buyer's financing can fall through due to last minute credit issues, job changes, or debt to income. Make sure your buyer is fully approved before you get to the closing table to avoid the risk of financing falling through. This is a common issue when buyers are pre-qualified with their lender instead of receiving approval (What to do after having a mortgage loan denied at closing, 2019).

Chapter Summary

- Buyers will conduct due diligence during their process, just like you.

- Conducting your due diligence will ensure you don't run into any issues during their due diligence.

- Be prepared for inspections and appraisals, and make sure you've done your homework for financing and that it's not held up.

- Make sure your buyer's financing is solid.

In the next chapter, you will learn about the closing.

Chapter Twenty: The Closing

The closing is the last part of your real estate deal. Once you reach the closing table, you are in the home stretch and one step closer to earning your first profit on a real estate deal. However, snags can come up at the closing table. That is why due diligence is so important. It helps to avoid any potential problems when you get this far down the road. There are several steps involved in the closing process. For your closing to be successful, none of these should be skipped.

- **Title insurance.** You will need to hire a title company to conduct a title search. More formally, "a title search is an examination of public records to determine and confirm a property's legal ownership and find out what claims, if any, exist on the property" (Seth, 2021).

- **Hire an attorney.** It is not required that you have an attorney present at the closing table, but it is highly recommended. A real estate attorney is going to be well-versed in the jargon and speech at the closing table. As a novice investor, it is important that you build strong allies with professionals that have more experience in this area than you do. Bring an attorney to the closing table.

- **Negotiate closing costs.** We have already covered negotiation earlier in this book. It is highly likely that your buyer will seek to have you cover closing costs in this deal. If you have done adequate preparation, you will know what you plan to cover, what you will not, and why. Stick to your plan.

- **Remove contingencies.** When you are sitting at the closing table, it's time to put a bow on the deal, and thus time to remove any contingencies that might exist with it. When you remove these contingencies, it must be stated in writing when these requests will be satisfied. For example, if you have repairs in a contingency, you must state when that repair will be completed.

- **Be prepared to sign a lot of paperwork.** If you've ever bought a home before, you know it comes with a lot of paperwork. This is no different; you are just on the seller side instead of the buyer side (Seth, 2021).

All money will be placed in escrow during the closing process to protect the interests of both the buyer and the seller. Once the closing process is complete, that money will be released from escrow. That is when you, our new investor friend, will get paid.

Chapter Summary

- The closing is the home stretch, but it is possible to run into snags.

- Follow the closing process to preserve your deal and profits.

Final Words

The world of house flipping and real estate investing is highly lucrative, but it is not something you should enter lightly. Contrary to what many people think, it is hard work and requires a significant investment of time and energy. Can you earn significant money as a house flipper? Absolutely! How much you earn will depend how much time and energy you want to put into it. As you can see, there are a lot of considerations when you are flipping a house. It's not a one-step process. It requires a lot of research. As a matter of fact, research is something you will spend a lot of your time doing. Without proper due diligence and knowledge of your market, you will end up making bad deals and even worse choices. The fact that you're reading this book is a good sign because this is step one of your due diligence. If you take the time to follow the steps in this book to acquire your first property, you've shown real commitment to the process.

It is advised that you don't skip any of the steps outlined in this book—not if you want to be a successful flipper. I understand if you thought you wouldn't have to manage anyone when you made the choice to become a real estate investor. But the reality is, yes, you will have to manage a team, that is, unless you plan to do all the work yourself, and we all know that is not the case. You will need to manage your team of contractors and it is important that you stay on them to manage your deadline. One way to combat this issue is to hire a general contractor. As we mentioned before, hiring a general contractor doesn't negate your responsibility as the investor. You still need to be onsite for the rehab. If you are still working during your flip, you are probably concerned about whether or not you can be present on site each day. That's where having a general contractor on site is even more valuable. You can have someone there serving as your eyes and ears when you can't be. But, even if you happen to have a demanding job that is keeping you from being on the site daily, make a point of being there at least a couple times a week. This is your flip, which means you should be invested in making sure that every aspect of the project goes as planned.

As a novice flipper, one of the most valuable things you can do is build allies and partnerships. We talked about networking and working with real estate agents earlier in this book. Early in your real estate career, this is extremely important because you want to glean from their expertise. As a new flipper, you are anxious to get involved with deals like distressed properties and foreclosures. But, we advise that you take your time in deals like this because their success hinges on experience. Build your network of partners and advisors and that will accelerate your growth as a new investor. The more you humble yourself and learn from their experience, the quicker you will move from a novice to an experienced investor. Plus, you will learn the value of a team around you as you grow in the business. Remember that old acronym for team—together, everyone accomplishes more. It's true.

Lastly, we advise that you take the time to build documents, like your scope of work. We understand that it's not fun and probably will feel like you're writing a report, but look at it as your blueprint to your flip. Think of it as a money document because that is exactly what it is. In real estate investing, the more prepared you are, the better. Building your scope of work forces you to think about the project and your anticipated outcomes. It lays out your plan and what you envision for the project. When you can start to build a vision for your project, it ignites your excitement for the project because then, you can learn more about what it can be. The most important thing to realize throughout this process is that it is not about you and your personal preferences. Part of your research is learning what the market wants and answering those needs. That is why we suggested that you tour the comps in your neighborhood to get a sense of what is trending and what the homes look like. You should build your finishes in your flip based on the information you learn from this process.

Not to beat a dead horse here, but like we said earlier, don't skip any steps. If you take the time to follow each step outlined in this book carefully, you will be well on your way to being a successful flipper. Take your time easing into the process. This is not an overnight process, but if you are steady and diligent, you will build a strong income as a real estate investor. Like we said earlier, don't try to do it all on your own. There is power in your team, and you want to leverage it to close as many deals as possible.

We are excited for you to accomplish your goals as a new real estate flipper. Now get out there and make some money!

If you enjoyed this book in anyway, an honest review is always appreciated!